ENGLISH FOR TODAY'S WORLD
with WORKBOOK

JOAN SASLOW
ALLEN ASCHER

Summit: English for Today's World   Level 1B with Workbook, Third Edition

Copyright © 2017 by Pearson Education, Inc.

All rights reserved. No part of this publication may be reproduced, stored in a retrieval system, or transmitted in any form or by any means, electronic, mechanical, photocopying, recording, or otherwise, without the prior permission of the publisher.

Pearson, 221 River Street, Hoboken, NJ 07030

Staff credits: The people who made up the *Summit* team representing editorial, production, design, manufacturing, and marketing are Pietro Alongi, Rhea Banker, Peter Benson, Stephanie Bullard, Jennifer Castro, Tracey Munz Cataldo, Rosa Chapinal, Aerin Csigay, Dave Dickey, Gina DiLillo, Christopher Leonowicz, Laurie Neaman, Alison Pei, Sherri Pemberton, Jennifer Raspiller, Mary Rich, Courtney Steers, Katherine Sullivan, and Paula Van Ells.

Cover credit: Tonis Pan/Shutterstock
Text composition: emc design ltd

Library of Congress Cataloging-in-Publication Data

Names: Saslow, Joan M., author. | Ascher, Allen, author.
Title: Summit : English for today's world / Joan Saslow and Allen Ascher.
Description: Third Edition. | White Plains, NY : Pearson Education, [2017]
Identifiers: LCCN 2016017942| ISBN 9780134096070 (book w/ CD) | ISBN 9780134176888 (book w/ CD) | ISBN 013409607X (book w/ CD)
Subjects: LCSH: English language--Textbooks for foreign speakers. | English language--Rhetoric. | English language--Sound recording for foreign speakers.
Classification: LCC PE1128 .S2757 2017 | DDC 428.2/4--dc23
LC record available at https://lccn.loc.gov/2016017942

Student Book

Photo credits: Original photography by Libby Ballengee/MPS. Page 62 (spider) Eric Isselee/Shutterstock, (bee) paulrommer/Shutterstock, (worm) Valentina Razumova/Shutterstock, (dolphin) FineShine/Shutterstock, (mouse) Tsekhmister/Shutterstock, (dog) Andresr/Shutterstock, (elephant) Richard Peterson/Shutterstock, (horse) Eric Isselee/Shutterstock, (lion) Eric Isselee/123 RF, (baboon) Eric Isselee/Shutterstock, (bunny) Joshua Lewis/Shutterstock, (sheep) Eric Isselee/Shutterstock, (parrot) Denis Tabler/Fotolia, (eagle) Eric Isselee/Shutterstock, (snake) Kruglov_Orda/Shutterstock, (crocodile) nattanan726/Shutterstock, (frog) Eric Isselee/Shutterstock, (salamander) Vitalii Hulai/Shuttersock, (eel) Eric Isselée/Fotolia, (goldfish) Gunnar Pippel/Shutterstock; p. 63 Ghislain & Marie David de Lossy/Cultura/Corbis; p. 64 (t) Joshua Rainey Photography/Shutterstock, (m) Suna/Fotolia, (b) Yanlev/Fotolia; p. 65 yulia-zl18/Fotolia; p. 66 (t) Tono Balaguer/123rf (b) Alena Ozerova/Shutterstock; p. 67 hin255/Shutterstock; (guinea pig) Inkwelldodo/Fotolia; p. 68 (top, left to right) Feng Yu/123rf, dazb75/Fotolia, Soren Egeberg Photography/Shutterstock, Meoita/Fotolia, (bottom, left to right) Valdecasas/Shutterstock, Lubos Chlubny/Fotolia, John Foxx/Getty Images, sbthegreenman/Fotolia; p. 69 (b) ARTENS/Fotolia; p. 70 (t) Jeff Foott. Alamy, (l) PARIS PIERCE/Alamy Stock Photo, (r) Everett Historical/Shutterstock; p. 75 Jupiterimages/Stockbyte/Getty Images; p. 77 Photosindia/Alamy Stock Photo; p. 78 (tl) Nicolas McComber/E+/Getty Images, (tr) DanielBendjy/E+/Getty Images, (bl) Rob Byron/Shutterstock, (br) Glow Images/Getty Images; p. 80 Tetra Images/Shutterstock; p. 86 bst2012/Fotolia; p. 87 Alistair Berg/DigitalVision/Getty Images; p. 88 Christin Lola/Shutterstock; p. 89 Monkey Business/Fotolia; p. 91 Jetta Productions/Blend Images/Getty Images; p. 92 (background) Anton Gvozdikov/Fotolia; (man) Syda Productions/Fotolia; p. 93 pressmaster/Fotolia; p. 94 (l) Robert Kneschke/Fotolia, (r) Monkey Business Images/Shutterstock; p. 95 (tl) Ana Bokan/Shutterstock, (r) Imtmphoto/Fotolia, (bl) Jim Pruitt/Shutterstock; p. 97 glisic albina/Fotolia; p. 98 (hat) cratervalley/fotolia, (canary) glifeisgood/Fotolia, (coin) MAC1/Shutterstock, (bird) kukies/Fotolia (arms) IgorGolovniov/Shutterstock; p. 99 (l) bokan/Fotolia, (r) DragonImages/Fotolia; p. 102 (l) Leksele/Shutterstock, (r) Everett Collection/Newscom; p. 103 (left to right) meunierd/Shutterstock, Pecold/Shutterstock, Jgz/Fotolia; p. 104 (top and bottom) aleciccotelli/Fotolia, (l) Cimmerian/Getty Images, photoBeard/ Shutterstock, (r) Oleg Prikhodko/Getty Images (right, inset) photoBeard/Shutterstock; p. 105 sss78/Fotolia; p. 106 Jeremy Craine/REX/Newscom; p. 107 michaeljung/Fotolia; p. 109 Monkey Business/Fotolia; p. 110 (fans) Chris Whitehead/Cultura/Getty Images, (skydivers) Joggie Botma/Shutterstock, (hammock) saras66/Shutterstock, (chess) auremar/Shutterstock; p. 113 Stockbroker/MBI / Alamy Stock Photo; p. 114 (t) Hurst Photo/Shutterstock, (m) khwanchai s/Fotolia, (b) Fotokvadrat/Fotolia; p. 115 paultarasenko/Fotolia; p. 116 Focus Pocus LTD/Fotolia; p. 117 Idprod/Fotolia; p. 118 (left to right) 2happy/Fotolia, creative soul/Fotolia, bikeriderlondon/Shutterstock, Maridav/Fotolia, Digital Vision/Getty Images; p. 119 Photocreo Bednarek/Fotolia; p. 138 Axel Bueckert/Fotolia (male), zea_lenanet/Fotolia (female).

Illustration credits: Aptara pp. 69, 74; Steve Attoe p. 90; Mark Collins pp. 65, (map, flag, camel, cat) 98; Francois Escalmel p. 83; Dusan Petricic pp. 100(b), 101; Shannon Wheelie p. 100(t); Liza Donnelley p. 76; Jerome Studer p. 81.

Workbook

Photo credits: 62: Gi0572/Fotolia; 67 (bottom): Kurhan/Fotolia; 67 (bottom, center): PT Images/Shutterstock; 67 (top): Felix Mizioznikov/Shutterstock; 67 (top, center): Rido/Fotolia; 68 (bottom, left): Pathdoc/Fotolia; 68 (bottom, right): Catherine Murray/Fotolia; 68 (top, left): Dglimages/Fotolia; 68 (top, right): Arek Malang/Shutterstock; 69: Delphotostock/Fotolia; 71: Minerva Studio/Fotolia; 72: Rocketclips/Fotolia; 79: Phattana/Fotolia; 84: Sergey Chirkov/Fotolia; 85: Xalanx/Fotolia; 91 (bottom): Pathdoc/Shutterstock; 91 (bottom, center): Piotr Marcinski/Fotolia; 91 (center): WavebreakmediaMicro/Fotolia; 91 (middle, center): Phovoir/Shutterstock; 91 (top): Bruno135_406/Fotolia; 91 (top, center): Carlos Caetano/Fotolia; 93: Mary Evans Picture Library/Alamy Stock Photo; 98: Kurapatka/Fotolia; 100 (bottom, left): Dwayne Foong/Fotolia; 100 (bottom, right): Asier Romero/Fotolia; 100 (center, left): Michael Spring/Fotolia; 100 (center, right): Siarhei Zapatylak/Fotolia; 100 (top, left): Elena Elisseeva/Shutterstock; 100 (top, right): Innovated Captures/Fotolia; 101: Mat Hayward/Fotolia.

Illustration credits: Leanne Franson, p. 89; ElectraGraphics, Inc. p. 57–58

Printed in the United States of America

ISBN-10: 0-13-449889-5
ISBN-13: 978-0-13-449889-8

pearsonelt.com/summit3e

Contents

Learning Objectives for 1A and 1B iv
To the Teacher viii
Components ix
About the Authors xi

UNIT 6	Animals	**62**
UNIT 7	Advertising and Consumers	**74**
UNIT 8	Family Trends	**86**
UNIT 9	Facts, Theories, and Hoaxes	**98**
UNIT 10	Your Free Time	**110**

Reference Charts 122
Grammar Booster 134
Pronunciation Booster 145
Test-Taking Skills Booster 156

WORKBOOK

UNIT 6	Animals	**W55**
UNIT 7	Advertising and Consumers	**W67**
UNIT 8	Family Trends	**W78**
UNIT 9	Facts, Theories, and Hoaxes	**W89**
UNIT 10	Your Free Time	**W98**

LEARNING OBJECTIVES

UNIT	COMMUNICATION GOALS	VOCABULARY	GRAMMAR
UNIT 1 **Outlook and Behavior** PAGE 2	• Describe your personality • Discuss someone's behavior • Compare perspectives on world problems • Discuss creative ways to achieve a goal	• Adjectives to describe personality traits **Word Study:** • Adjective suffixes -ful and -less	• Gerunds and infinitives: review and expansion • Verbs that require a noun or pronoun before an infinitive **GRAMMAR BOOSTER** • Infinitives: review, expansion, and common errors • Grammar for writing: parallelism with gerunds and infinitives
UNIT 2 **Music and Other Arts** PAGE 14	• Describe how you've been enjoying the arts • Express a negative opinion politely • Describe a creative personality • Discuss the benefits of the arts	• Elements of music • Negative descriptions of music • Describing creative personalities **Word Study:** • Using participial adjectives	• The present perfect continuous • Cleft sentences with What **GRAMMAR BOOSTER** • Finished and unfinished actions: summary • Noun clauses: review and expansion • Grammar for Writing: noun clauses as adjective and noun complements
UNIT 3 **Money, Finance, and You** PAGE 26	• Express buyer's remorse • Talk about financial goals and plans • Discuss good and bad money management • Explain reasons for charitable giving	• Describing spending styles • Expressing buyer's remorse • Good and bad money management **Word Study:** • Parts of speech	• Expressing regrets about the past: wish + past perfect; should have / ought to have + past participle; if only + past perfect. • Completed future actions and plans: The future perfect and perfect infinitives **GRAMMAR BOOSTER** • The past unreal conditional: inverted form • The future continuous • The future perfect continuous
UNIT 4 **Clothing and Appearance** PAGE 38	• Describe clothing details and formality • Talk about changes in clothing customs • Examine questionable cosmetic procedures • Discuss appearance and self-esteem	• Adjectives to describe fashion • Describing clothes **Word Study:** • Compound words with self-	• Quantifiers: review and expansion **GRAMMAR BOOSTER** • A few / few; a little / little • Quantifiers: using of for specific reference • Quantifiers used without referents • Grammar for Writing: subject-verb agreement of quantifiers followed by of
UNIT 5 **Communities** PAGE 50	• Politely ask someone not to do something • Complain about public conduct • Suggest ways to avoid being a victim of urban crime • Discuss the meaning of community	• Types of locations • Community service activities **Word Study:** • Using negative prefixes to form antonyms	• Possessive gerunds • Paired conjunctions **GRAMMAR BOOSTER** • Conjunctions with so, too, neither, or not either • So, too, neither, or not either: short responses

CONVERSATION STRATEGIES	LISTENING / PRONUNCIATION	READING	WRITING
• Use I'd say to soften an assertive opinion • Use I don't see [myself] that way to politely contradict another's statement • Say I see [you] as to explain your own point of view • Use tend to and seem to to make generalizations	• Listen to activate grammar • Listen to classify • Listen for main ideas • Listen for details • Understand meaning from context **PRONUNCIATION BOOSTER** • Content words and function words	**Texts:** • A survey about positive and negative outlooks • Descriptions of other people's behavior • A newspaper article about a creative solution to a problem **Skills / strategies:** • Understand idioms and expressions • Determine the main idea • Understand meaning from context • Summarize	**Task:** • Write about your outlook on a world problem **Skill:** • Paragraph structure: Review
• Use To tell the truth, To be honest, and I hate to say it, but to politely introduce a contrary opinion	• Listen to activate vocabulary • Listen for main ideas • Listen for supporting information • Listen to take notes • Listen for details **PRONUNCIATION BOOSTER** • Intonation patterns	**Texts:** • A survey about musical memories • Commentaries about enjoying the arts • A short biography **Skills / strategies:** • Understand idioms and expressions • Infer information • Identify supporting details • Express and support an opinion	**Task:** • Describe your interests and personality **Skill:** • Parallel structure
• Use You know, … to introduce a new topic of conversation • Use I hate to say it, but to introduce negative information • Ask What do you mean? to invite someone to elaborate • Say That's a shame to show empathy • Say I'll think about that when you're non-committal about someone's suggestion	• Listen for details • Listen to activate vocabulary • Listen to confirm content • Listen to summarize • Listen to evaluate **PRONUNCIATION BOOSTER** • Sentence rhythm: thought groups	**Texts:** • A spending habits self-test • Interview responses about financial goals • A guide to charitable giving **Skills / strategies:** • Understand idioms and expressions • Understand meaning from context • Draw conclusions • Express and support an opinion	**Task:** • Write a personal statement about how you manage financial responsibilities **Skill:** • Organizing information by degrees of importance
• Use Can I ask you a question about…? to introduce a subject you are unsure of • Use I mean to elaborate on a prior statement or question • Use Actually, to assert a point of view • Begin a question with So to affirm understanding of someone's earlier statement • Say I think that might be … to gently warn that something is inappropriate	• Listen for main ideas • Listen for details • Listen to summarize **PRONUNCIATION BOOSTER** • Linking sounds	**Texts:** • Descriptions of personal style • An article about the evolution of "business casual" attire • An article about questionable cosmetic procedures • Advertisements for cosmetic procedures **Skills / strategies:** • Understand idioms and expressions • Understand meaning from context • Identify supporting details • Express and support an opinion	**Task:** • Write two paragraphs comparing tastes in fashion **Skill:** • Compare and contrast: Review
• Use Do you mind…? to ask permission to do something • Use Not at all to affirm that you are not bothered or inconvenienced • Use That's very [considerate] of you to thank someone for accommodating you	• Listen to summarize • Listen for details • Listen to confirm content • Listen to infer **PRONUNCIATION BOOSTER** • Unstressed syllables: vowel reduction to /ə/	**Texts:** • A questionnaire about community • Interview responses about pet peeves • A magazine article about urban crime • A website about community projects **Skills / strategies:** • Understand idioms and expressions • Classify • Understand meaning from context • Critical thinking	**Task:** • Write a formal letter of complaint **Skill:** • Formal letters: Review

UNIT	COMMUNICATION GOALS	VOCABULARY	GRAMMAR
UNIT 6 **Animals** PAGE 62	• Exchange opinions about the treatment of animals • Discuss the pros and cons of certain pets • Compare animal and human behavior • Debate the value of animal conservation	• Categories of animals • Describing pets • Animal social groups and physical features	• Passive modals **GRAMMAR BOOSTER** • Modals and modal-like expressions: summary
UNIT 7 **Advertising and Consumers** PAGE 74	• Evaluate ways and places to shop • Discuss your reactions to ads • Discuss problem shopping behavior • Persuade someone to buy a product	• Verbs for shopping activities • Ways to persuade	• Passive forms of gerunds and infinitives **GRAMMAR BOOSTER** • The passive voice: review and expansion
UNIT 8 **Family Trends** PAGE 86	• Describe family trends • Discuss parent-teen issues • Compare generations • Discuss caring for the elderly	• Describing parent and teen behavior **Word Study:** • Transforming verbs and adjectives into nouns	• Repeated comparatives and double comparatives **GRAMMAR BOOSTER** • Making comparisons: review and expansion • Other uses of comparatives, superlatives, and comparisons with as…as
UNIT 9 **Facts, Theories, and Hoaxes** PAGE 98	• Speculate about everyday situations • Present a theory • Discuss how believable a story is • Evaluate the trustworthiness of news sources	• Degrees of certainty **Word Study:** • Adjectives with the suffix -able	• Perfect modals for speculating about the past: active and passive voice **GRAMMAR BOOSTER** • Perfect modals: short responses (active and passive voice)
UNIT 10 **Your Free Time** PAGE 110	• Suggest ways to reduce stress • Describe how you got interested in a hobby • Discuss how mobile devices affect us • Compare attitudes about taking risks	• Ways to describe people • Ways to reduce stress **Word Study:** • Adverbs of manner	• Expressing an expectation with be supposed to • Describing past repeated or habitual actions: would and the past continuous with always **GRAMMAR BOOSTER** • Be supposed to: expansion • Would: review • Grammar for Writing: placement of adverbs of manner

Reference Charts .... page 122
Grammar Booster .... page 134
Pronunciation Booster .... page 145
Test-Taking Skills Booster .... page 156

CONVERSATION STRATEGIES	LISTENING / PRONUNCIATION	READING	WRITING
• Use I've heard to introduce a commonly-held belief or opinion • Respond with In what way? to request further explanation • Use For one thing to introduce a first supporting argument • Use And besides to add another supporting argument • Use But what if to suggest a hypothetical situation	• Listen to activate vocabulary • Listen to define terms • Listen for examples • Listen for details **PRONUNCIATION BOOSTER** • Sound reduction	**Texts:** • Social media posts about treatment of animals • An article about animal conservation **Skills / strategies:** • Understand idioms and expressions • Understand meaning from context • Recognize cause and effect	**Task:** • Write a persuasive essay about the treatment of animals **Skill:** • Supporting a point of view
• Say Quick question to indicate one wants some simple information • Introduce an opinion with I find • Say That's good to know to express satisfaction for information • Use Why don't you… to offer advice	• Listen to activate vocabulary • Listen to infer **PRONUNCIATION BOOSTER** • Vowel sounds /i/ and /ɪ/	**Texts:** • Self-tests about shopping mistakes and behavior • Descriptions of techniques used in advertising • Interview responses about compulsive shopping **Skills / strategies:** • Understand idioms and expressions • Understand meaning from context • Identify supporting details	**Task:** • Write a summary of an article **Skill:** • Summarize and paraphrase someone's point of view
• Ask Why's that? to ask someone to elaborate on an opinion • Say I suppose, but … to signal partial agreement	• Listen to activate grammar • Listen to activate vocabulary • Listen for supporting information • Listen for details • Listen to compare and contrast **PRONUNCIATION BOOSTER** • Stress placement: prefixes and suffixes	**Texts:** • A survey about parents and teens • A brochure about falling birthrates • A report on the increase in global population of older people **Skills / strategies:** • Understand idioms and expressions • Summarize • Understand meaning from context • Critical thinking • Draw conclusions	**Task:** • Write a blog post of three or more paragraphs about advice for parents and teens **Skill:** • Avoiding run-on sentences and comma splices
• Use I wonder to introduce something you're not sure about • Say I'm sure it's nothing to indicate that something is probably not serious • Say I suppose you're right to acknowledge someone's point of view • Say There must be a good explanation to assure someone that things will turn out OK	• Listen to activate vocabulary • Listen for main ideas • Listen to draw conclusions **PRONUNCIATION BOOSTER** • Reduction and linking in perfect modals in the passive voice	**Texts:** • A quiz about tricky facts • An article about Rapa Nui • Facts and theories about mysteries • An article about a UFO conspiracy theory • A survey about the trustworthiness of information sources **Skills / strategies:** • Understand idioms and expressions • Confirm point of view • Infer information	**Task:** • Write a news article about a mysterious event **Skill:** • Avoiding sentence fragments
• Say Uh-oh to indicate that you realize you've made a mistake • Use I just realized to acknowledge a mistake • Use Well, frankly to indicate that you are going to be honest about something • Use It's just that or Let's face it to introduce an honest criticism or assessment • Use You know what? to introduce a piece of advice	• Listen to activate vocabulary • Listen for main ideas • Listen for supporting details • Listen to understand meaning from context **PRONUNCIATION BOOSTER** • Vowel sounds /eɪ/, /ɛ/, /æ/, and /ʌ/	**Texts:** • A survey about free time • Descriptions of how people got interested in their hobbies • An article about the impact of mobile devices • A survey about mobile device usage **Skills / strategies:** • Understand idioms and expressions • Understand meaning from context • Identify supporting details • Infer point of view	**Task:** • Write a critique of an article **Skill:** • Presenting and supporting opinions clearly

TO THE TEACHER

What is *Summit*?

Summit is a two-level high-intermediate to advanced communicative course that develops confident, culturally fluent English speakers able to navigate the social, travel, and professional situations they will encounter as they use English in their lives. *Summit* can follow the intermediate level of any communicative series, including the four-level *Top Notch* course.

Summit delivers immediate, demonstrable results in every class session through its proven pedagogy and systematic and intensive recycling of language. Each goal- and achievement-based lesson is tightly correlated to the Can-Do Statements of the Common European Framework of Reference (CEFR). The course is fully benchmarked to the Global Scale of English (GSE).

Each level of *Summit* contains material for 60 to 90 hours of classroom instruction. Its full array of additional print and digital components can extend instruction to 120 hours if desired. Furthermore, the entire *Summit* course can be tailored to blended learning with its integrated online component, *MyEnglishLab*. *Summit* offers more ready-to-use teacher resources than any other course available today.

NEW This third edition represents a major revision of content and has a greatly increased quantity of exercises, both print and digital. Following are some key new features:

- **Conversation Activator Videos** to build communicative competence
- **Discussion Activator Videos** to increase quality and quantity of expression
- A **Test-Taking Skills Booster** (and **Extra Challenge Reading Activities**) to help students succeed in the reading and listening sections of standardized tests
- An **Understand Idioms and Expressions** section in each unit increases the authenticity of student spoken language

Award-Winning Instructional Design*

Demonstrable confirmation of progress
Every two-page lesson has a clearly stated communication goal and culminates in a guided conversation, free discussion, debate, presentation, role play, or project that achieves the goal. Idea framing and notepadding activities lead students to confident spoken expression.

Cultural fluency
Summit audio familiarizes students with a wide variety of native and non-native accents. Discussion activities reflect the topics people of diverse cultural backgrounds talk about in their social and professional lives.

Explicit vocabulary and grammar
Clear captioned illustrations and dictionary-style presentations, all with audio, take the guesswork out of meaning and ensure comprehensible pronunciation. Grammar is embedded in context and presented explicitly for form, meaning, and use. The unique "Recycle this Language" feature encourages active use of newly learned words and grammar during communication practice.

Active listening syllabus
More than 50 listening tasks at each level of *Summit* develop critical thinking and crucial listening comprehension skills such as listen for details, main ideas, confirmation of content, inference, and understand meaning from context.

**Summit is the recipient of the Association of Educational Publishers' Distinguished Achievement Award.*

Conversation and Discussion Activators
Memorable conversation models with audio provide appealing natural social language and conversation strategies essential for post-secondary learners. Rigorous Conversation Activator and Discussion Activator activities with video systematically stimulate recycling of social language, ensuring it is not forgotten. A unique Pronunciation Booster provides lessons and interactive practice, with audio, so students can improve their spoken expression.

Systematic writing skills development
Summit teaches the conventions of correct English writing so students will be prepared for standardized tests, academic study, and professional communication. Lessons cover key writing and rhetorical skills such as using parallel structure and avoiding sentence fragments, run-on sentences, and comma splices. Intensive work in paragraph and essay development ensures confident and successful writing.

Reading skills and strategies
Each unit of *Summit* builds critical thinking and key reading skills and strategies such as paraphrasing, drawing conclusions, expressing and supporting an opinion, and activating prior knowledge. Learners develop analytical skills and increase fluency while supporting their answers through speaking.

We wish you and your students enjoyment and success with **Summit**. *We wrote it for you.*
Joan Saslow and Allen Ascher

COMPONENTS

ActiveTeach

Maximize the impact of your *Summit* lessons. Digital Student's Book pages with access to all audio and video provide an interactive classroom experience that can be used with or without an interactive whiteboard (IWB). It includes a full array of easy-to-access digital and printable features.

For class presentation . . .

- 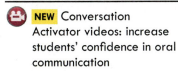 **NEW** Conversation Activator videos: increase students' confidence in oral communication
- 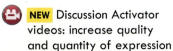 **NEW** Discussion Activator videos: increase quality and quantity of expression
-  **NEW** Extra Grammar Exercises: ensure mastery of grammar
- **NEW** Extra Challenge Reading Activities: help students succeed at standardized proficiency tests.

PLUS

- Interactive Whiteboard tools, including zoom, highlight, links, notes, and more.
- Clickable Audio: instant access to the complete classroom audio program
- *Summit TV* Video Program: fully-revised authentic TV documentaries as well as unscripted on-the-street interviews, featuring a variety of regional and non-native accents

For planning . . .

- A *Methods Handbook* for a communicative classroom
- Detailed timed lesson plans for each two-page lesson
- *Summit TV* teaching notes
- Complete answer keys, audio scripts, and video scripts

For extra support . . .

- Hundreds of extra printable activities, with teaching notes
- *Summit TV* activity worksheets

For assessment . . .

- Ready-made unit and review achievement tests with options to edit, add, or delete items.

Ready-made Summit Web Projects provide authentic application of lesson language.

MyEnglishLab
An optional online learning tool

- **NEW** Immediate, meaningful feedback on wrong answers
- **NEW** Remedial grammar exercises
- **NEW** Grammar Coach videos for general reference
- Interactive practice of all material presented in the course
- Grade reports that display performance and time on task
- Auto-graded achievement tests

Workbook
Lesson-by-lesson written exercises to accompany the Student's Book

Full-Course Placement Tests
Choose printable or online version

Classroom Audio Program

- A set of Audio CDs, as an alternative to the clickable audio in ActiveTeach
- Contains a variety of authentic regional and non-native accents to build comprehension of diverse English speakers
- **NEW** The app *Summit Go* allows access anytime, anywhere and lets students practice at their own pace. The entire audio program is also available for students at www.english.com/summit3e.

Teacher's Edition and Lesson Planner

- Detailed interleaved lesson plans, language and culture notes, answer keys, and more
- Also accessible in digital form in ActiveTeach

For more information: www.pearsonelt.com/summit3e

ABOUT THE AUTHORS

Joan Saslow

Joan Saslow has taught in a variety of programs in South America and the United States. She is author or coauthor of a number of widely used courses, some of which are *Ready to Go*, *Workplace Plus*, *Literacy Plus*, and *Top Notch*. She is also author of *English in Context*, a series for reading science and technology. Ms. Saslow was the series director of *True Colors* and *True Voices*. She has participated in the English Language Specialist Program in the U.S. Department of State's Bureau of Educational and Cultural Affairs.

Allen Ascher

Allen Ascher has been a teacher and teacher trainer in China and the United States, as well as academic director of the intensive English program at Hunter College. Mr. Ascher has also been an ELT publisher and was responsible for publication and expansion of numerous well-known courses including *True Colors*, *NorthStar*, the *Longman TOEFL Preparation Series*, and the *Longman Academic Writing Series*. He is coauthor of *Top Notch*, and he wrote the "Teaching Speaking" module of *Teacher Development Interactive*, an online multimedia teacher-training program.

Ms. Saslow and Mr. Ascher are frequent presenters at professional conferences and have been coauthoring courses for teens, adults, and young adults since 2002.

AUTHORS' ACKNOWLEDGMENTS

The authors wish to thank Katherine Klagsbrun for developing the digital Extra Challenge Reading Activities that appear with all reading selections in *Summit 1*.

The authors are indebted to these reviewers, who provided extensive and detailed feedback and suggestions for *Summit*, as well as the hundreds of teachers who completed surveys and participated in focus groups.

Cris Asperti, CEL LEP, São Paulo, Brazil • **Diana Alicia Ávila Martínez**, CUEC, Monterrey, Mexico • **Shannon Brown**, Nagoya University of Foreign Studies, Nagoya, Japan • **Cesar Byrd**, Universidad ETAC Campus Chalco, Mexico City, Mexico • **Maria Claudia Campos de Freitas**, Metalanguage, São Paulo, Brazil • **Alvaro Del Castillo Alba**, CBA, Santa Cruz, Bolivia • **Isidro Castro Galván**, Instituto Teocalli, Monterrey, Mexico • **Melisa Celi**, Idiomas Católica, Lima, Peru • **Carlos Celis**, CEL LEP, São Paulo, Brazil • **Jussara Costa e Silva**, Prize Language School, São Paulo, Brazil • **Inara Couto**, CEL LEP, São Paulo, Brazil • **Gemma Crouch**, ICPNA Chiclayo, Peru • **Ingrid Valverde Diaz del Olmo**, ICPNA Cusco, Peru • **Jacqueline Díaz Esquivel**, PROULEX, Guadalajara, Mexico • **María Eid Ceneviva**, CBA, Cochabamba, Bolivia • **Erika Licia Esteves Silva**, Murphy English, São Paulo, Brazil • **Cristian Garay**, Idiomas Católica, Lima, Peru • **Miguel Angel Guerrero Pozos**, PROULEX, Guadalajara, Mexico • **Anderson Francisco Guimarães Maia**, Centro Cultural Brasil Estados Unidos, Belém, Brazil • **Cesar Guzmán**, CAADI Monterrey, Mexico • **César Iván Hernández Escobedo**, PROULEX, Guadalajara, Mexico • **Robert Hinton**, Nihon University, Tokyo, Japan • **Segundo Huanambal Díaz**, ICPNA Chiclayo, Peru • **Chandra Víctor Jacobs Sukahai**, Universidad de Valle de México, Monterrey, Mexico • **Yeni Jiménez Torres**, Centro Colombo Americano Bogotá, Colombia • **Simon Lees**, Nagoya University of Foreign Studies, Nagoya, Japan • **Thomas LeViness**, PROULEX, Guadalajara, Mexico • **Amy Lewis**, Waseda University, Tokyo, Japan • **Luz Libia Rey**, Centro Colombo Americano, Bogotá, Colombia • **Diego López**, Idiomas Católica, Lima, Peru • **Junior Lozano**, Idiomas Católica, Lima, Peru • **Tanja McCandie**, Nanzan University, Nagoya, Japan • **Tammy Martínez Nieves**, Universidad Autónoma de Nuevo León, Monterrey, Mexico • **María Teresa Meléndez Mantilla**, ICPNA Chiclayo, Peru • **Mónica Nomberto**, ICPNA Chiclayo, Peru • **Otilia Ojeda**, Monterrey, Mexico • **Juana Palacios**, Idiomas Católica, Lima, Peru • **Giuseppe Paldino Mayorga**, Jellyfish Learning Center, San Cristobal, Ecuador • **Henry Eduardo Pardo Lamprea**, Universidad Militar Nueva Granada, Colombia • **Dario Paredes**, Centro Colombo Americano, Bogotá, Colombia • **Teresa Noemí Parra Alarcón**, Centro Anglo Americano de Cuernavaca, S.C., Cuernavaca, Mexico • **Carlos Eduardo de la Paz Arroyo**, Centro Anglo Americano de Cuernavaca, S.C., Cuernavaca, Mexico • **José Luis Pérez Treviño**, Instituto Obispado, Monterrey, Mexico • **Evelize Maria Plácido Florian**, São Paulo, Brazil • **Armida Rivas**, Monterrey, Mexico • **Luis Rodríguez Amau**, ICPNA Chiclayo, Peru • **Fabio Ossaamn Rok Kaku**, Prize Language School, São Paulo, Brazil • **Ana María Román Villareal**, CUEC, Monterrey, Mexico • **Reynaldo Romano C.**, CBA, La Paz, Bolivia • **Francisco Rondón**, Centro Colombo Americano, Bogotá, Colombia • **Peter Russell**, Waseda University, Tokyo, Japan • **Rubena St. Louis**, Universidad Simón Bolivar, Caracas, Venezuela • **Marisol Salazar**, Centro Colombo Americano, Bogotá, Colombia • **Miguel Sierra**, Idiomas Católica, Lima, Peru • **Greg Strong**, Aoyama Gakuin University, Tokyo, Japan • **Gerald Talandis**, Toyama University, Toyama, Japan • **Stephen Thompson**, Nagoya University of Foreign Studies, Nagoya, Japan • **José Luis Urbina Hurtado**, Instituto Tecnológico de León, Mexico • **René F. Valdivia Pereyra**, CBA, Santa Cruz, Bolivia • **Magno Alejandro Vivar Hurtado**, Salesian Polytechnic University, Ecuador • **Belkis Yanes**, Caracas, Venezuela • **Holger Zamora**, ICPNA Cusco, Peru • **Maria Cristina Zanon Costa**, Metalanguage, São Paulo, Brazil • **Kathia Zegarra**, Idiomas Católica, Lima, Peru.

UNIT 6 Animals

COMMUNICATION GOALS
1. Exchange opinions about the treatment of animals
2. Discuss the pros and cons of certain pets
3. Compare animal and human behavior
4. Debate the value of animal conservation

PREVIEW

A **FRAME YOUR IDEAS** Complete the activity. With a partner, explain your choices. Which categories of animals invite the most negative or positive responses?

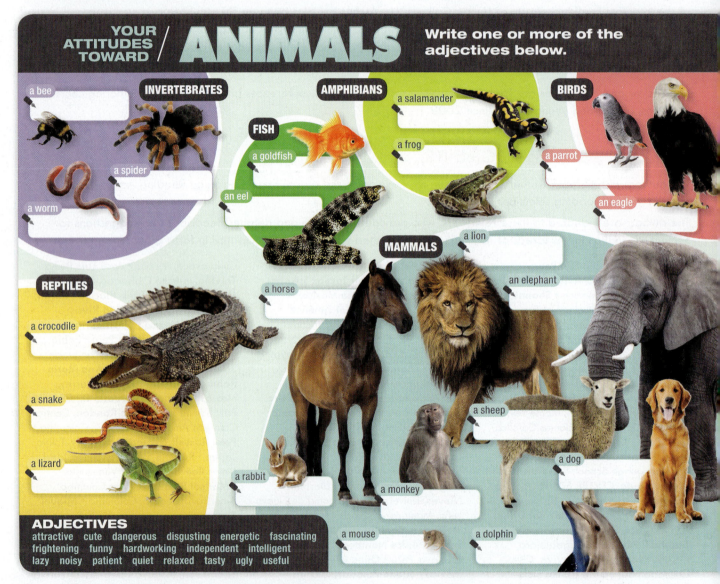

YOUR ATTITUDES TOWARD ANIMALS — Write one or more of the adjectives below.

INVERTEBRATES: a bee, a spider, a worm
FISH: a goldfish, an eel
AMPHIBIANS: a salamander, a frog
BIRDS: a parrot, an eagle
REPTILES: a crocodile, a snake, a lizard
MAMMALS: a horse, a lion, an elephant, a rabbit, a monkey, a sheep, a dog, a mouse, a dolphin

ADJECTIVES
attractive cute dangerous disgusting energetic fascinating
frightening funny hardworking independent intelligent
lazy noisy patient quiet relaxed tasty ugly useful

B ▶ 3:14 **VOCABULARY   CATEGORIES OF ANIMALS** Look at the categories and photos in Exercise A. Listen and repeat.

C **DISCUSSION** Discuss the questions.
1. Would your responses have been different if any of the animals had been babies instead of adults? How?
2. Did any other physical factors affect your choices, such as color or size? In what ways?
3. Did any experiences you've had with any of these animals affect your choices? How?

D ▶ 3:15 **SPOTLIGHT** Read and listen to a conversation over lunch at an international meeting. Notice the spotlighted language.

ENGLISH FOR TODAY'S WORLD
Understand a variety of accents.
Pam = Australian English
Karina = German

Pam: Nice picture. Hey, are those your cats?
Karina: Yeah, they're my babies. We've had the gray one a long time. She's almost seventeen now.
Pam: No way! She still looks so healthy. What about the white one?
Karina: We think he's pretty young. Actually, he was hanging around outside our house all summer, and it didn't seem like anyone was taking care of him. We **felt sorry for** him, so we took him in.
Pam: Lucky cat! He looks like a member of the family now. But I'll bet the older one wasn't too crazy about having a new cat around.
Karina: Well, he thinks he's still a kitten; he just wants to play all the time. But I'd say she **puts up with** him pretty well. She's really patient.
Pam: From the picture, it looks like she's the one **in charge**.
Karina: Definitely. She doesn't fool around. If he gets too rough, she knows how to **put him in his place**. Hey, do you have any pets?
Pam: No, we don't. When we feel like being around animals, we go to the zoo.
Karina: Actually, I'm not too crazy about zoos. I just don't think animals should be **cooped up** in small cages.
Pam: Normally I'd agree with you. But our local zoo isn't like that at all. The larger mammals have plenty of outdoor space. It's pretty humane, I think.
Karina: Well, that's good. I guess we shouldn't just assume that animals in captivity aren't treated well.

E **UNDERSTAND IDIOMS AND EXPRESSIONS** Find each expression in Spotlight. Then complete the statements.

1 When Karina says they "felt sorry for" the younger cat, she means they ...... him.
  a apologized to   b were concerned about   c were annoyed with

2 When she says the older cat "puts up with" the younger one, she means the older cat ....
  a is annoyed with him   b accepts his behavior   c is concerned about him

3 When she says the gray cat is the one "in charge," she means the gray cat ....
  a obeys the white one   b is obeyed by the white one   c is older than the white one

4 When she says the gray cat put the white one "in his place," she means the gray one ....
  a is the boss   b isn't the boss   c is his friend

5 When she refers to animals being "cooped up in" cages, she means they ....
  a are made comfortable   b don't get to go outside   c often go outdoors

F **PAIR WORK** Choose one or more of these topics. Tell your partner about:
• a time when you or someone you know felt sorry for an animal and took it in.
• a time when someone's pet had to put up with another animal.
• a home where the pet was the one in charge.

SPEAKING **GROUP WORK** Discuss the questions.
1 Do you care if an animal is cooped up in a cage? Why or why not? Are there times when an animal should be?
2 Which animals on page 62 do you think need lots of outdoor space? Why?

LESSON 1

GOAL Exchange opinions about the treatment of animals

A ▶ 3:16 **GRAMMAR SPOTLIGHT** Read the social media posts. Notice the **spotlighted** grammar.

David Suchet — June 30 / Seattle, USA

I really feel sorry for animals that are mistreated. Does anyone else get as fed up as I do about their inhumane treatment? In my opinion, animals **should** never **be killed** just for sport or entertainment. Hunting, bullfighting, and any other "sport" that involves the killing of defenseless animals **should be** completely **banned**. And the idea that monkeys or dogs **have to be used** in medical research seems ridiculous to me. What do you all think? Is inhumane treatment of animals ever justified?

Reiko Yamamoto — July 1 / Atami, Japan

Maybe you're right about killing animals for sport, but don't you think the needs of people **should** sometimes **be considered**? For example, it seems clear to me that small mammals like mice or rabbits **have to be used** for medical research to make sure new medications are safe. It just **can't be avoided**. Otherwise, new medical treatments **might not be discovered**. We can't fool around when it comes to medicine.

Marie Colbert — July 1 / Lyon, France

I agree with Reiko—people first. But that doesn't mean animals **should be treated** inhumanely. I'm sure research methods **could be improved**. And recently I was reading about factory farms that raise chickens or beef cattle, and I was shocked at how crowded and filthy the conditions were. I know animals **have to be slaughtered** for food, but I'm sure they **could be raised** more humanely.

B **EVALUATE IDEAS** Do you agree with any of the opinions expressed in the posts? Why or why not?

> **GRAMMAR BOOSTER** p. 134
> • Modals and modal-like expressions: summary

C **GRAMMAR** **PASSIVE MODALS**

Remember: We use the passive voice to focus on the receiver of an action rather than the person or thing that performs the action. Form passive modals with a modal + <u>be</u> and a past participle.

Conditions for cattle on factory farms	**could**	**be improved**.
Alternatives to using mice for research	**might**	**be found**.
The hunting of bears	**should**	**be prohibited**.
Traditions like bullfighting	**have to***	**be preserved**.

*Note: <u>Have to</u> is a modal-like expression, not a true modal. It has two present forms: <u>have</u> and <u>has</u>. It uses <u>Do</u> or <u>Does</u> in questions and <u>don't</u> and <u>doesn't</u> in negative statements.

Yes / no questions
- **Should** chickens **be cooped up** in cages?
- **Can't** factory chicken farms **be shut down**?
- BUT **Do** large mammals **have to be kept** in zoos?

Information questions
- Why **shouldn't** reptiles or amphibians **be used** for research?
- Why **must** all animals' lives **be respected**?
- How **might** people's attitudes **be changed**?

Remember:
have to = obligatory
don't have to = not obligatory
must OR **must not** = obligatory

D NOTICE THE GRAMMAR   Find one passive modal in Spotlight on page 63.

E UNDERSTAND THE GRAMMAR   With a partner, decide who the performer of the action is. Then choose the active or passive voice to complete each statement.
1 People (should treat / should be treated) animals humanely.
2 Large mammals like lions (shouldn't keep / shouldn't be kept) in zoos.
3 In order to help people with disabilities, dogs (have to train / have to be trained) when they are young.
4 They say people (can teach / can be taught) bears to do tricks like dancing or standing up on command.
5 Horses (shouldn't force / shouldn't be forced) to run in races.
6 Sometimes, in order to protect people, aggressive dogs that live on the street (have to kill / have to be killed).

In item 1, people is the performer of the action.

F GRAMMAR PRACTICE   Write sentences, using passive modals.
1 People / shouldn't / allow to hunt elephants. ....
2 New medicines / might / discover through animal research. ....
3 Monkeys / shouldn't / keep as pets. ....
4 A lot / could / do to improve conditions for cattle on factory farms. ....
5 The treatment of research animals / must / improve. ....
6 Can't / zoos / use for performing scientific research to protect animals? ....
7 Why / chickens / have to / raise in such crowded conditions? ....

NOW YOU CAN   Exchange opinions about the treatment of animals

A DISCUSSION ACTIVATOR   Use the ideas to exchange opinions with a partner about the ways animals are used or treated. Ask and answer questions, using passive modals. Say as much as you can.

*Do you think animals **have to be used** for medical research? I do. We can't experiment on humans, can we?*

*Actually, I don't think animals **should be treated** that way. I think it's morally wrong.*

Ideas
- using animals in medical research
- slaughtering animals for food
- keeping animals in zoos
- raising animals for sports, such as racing or fighting
- killing animals for their hides and fur

a fur coat

RECYCLE THIS LANGUAGE

Express an opinion
- I think [it's morally wrong].
- I believe [it's OK under some circumstances].
- I feel [it's wrong no matter what].
- I'm in favor of ___ .
- I'm opposed to ___ .

Disagree
- I see what you mean, but ___ .
- That's one way to look at it, but ___ .
- On the one hand ___ , but on the other hand ___ .
- I completely disagree.

Agree
- I couldn't agree with you more.
- I completely agree.
- You're so right.

B SUMMARIZE THE DISCUSSION   Compare your classmates' opinions about the treatment of animals. Does the majority of the class share the same opinions?

LESSON 2

GOAL Discuss the pros and cons of certain pets

A ▶ 3:17 VOCABULARY DESCRIBING PETS Read and listen. Then listen again and repeat.

Positive traits	
playful	active and fun-loving
affectionate	friendly and loving
gentle / good-natured	easygoing; good with kids and other pets
low-maintenance	easy to care for and inexpensive to keep
loyal / devoted	attentive to its owner; reliable
protective	good at protecting its owner from danger

Negative traits	
high-strung / excitable	nervous; easily frightened
costly	expensive to buy and to take care of
destructive	harmful to furniture and other things
filthy	unclean; makes a mess
high-maintenance	time-consuming to take care of
aggressive	hard to control; possibly dangerous

Puppies are great for kids because they're affectionate and playful. However, they're also high maintenance.

B ▶ 3:18 LISTEN TO ACTIVATE VOCABULARY Listen to each conversation and complete the chart with the pet and its pros and cons. Use the Vocabulary. Listen again if necessary.

	Pet	Possible pros	Possible cons
1			
2			
3			
4			

C EXPRESS AND SUPPORT AN OPINION
Discuss the questions.

1. In what ways can an animal be a good companion to a child? An adult? An older person?
2. Do you know anyone who is too attached to his or her pet? Why do you think some people get emotionally close to their animals?

D GROUP WORK Use the vocabulary to tell your classmates about your past or present pets or about those of people you know.

PRONUNCIATION BOOSTER p. 145
Sound reduction

66 UNIT 6

NOW YOU CAN Discuss the pros and cons of certain pets

A ▶ 3:19 **CONVERSATION SPOTLIGHT** Read and listen. Notice the spotlighted conversation strategies.

A: Do you think a poodle would make a good pet?
B: Actually, I'm not so sure. **I've heard** they're really high-maintenance.
A: **In what way?**
B: Well, **for one thing**, they need a lot of attention. I'd consider getting a guinea pig instead.
A: Why a guinea pig?
B: Well, they're very low-maintenance. **And besides,** they're really gentle.
A: **But what if** you were looking for something a bit more affectionate than a guinea pig?
B: Then I'd get a cat. They're affectionate *and* they're low-maintenance.

a poodle

a guinea pig

B ▶ 3:20 **RHYTHM AND INTONATION** Listen again and repeat. Then practice the conversation with a partner.

C **NOTEPADDING** With a partner, complete the chart with animals that make good and bad pets. Explain why, using the Vocabulary. Choose animals from page 62 or others you know.

Animals that make exceptionally good pets	Reasons

Animals that make really bad pets	Reasons

D **CONVERSATION ACTIVATOR**
Create a conversation similar to the one in Exercise A, using the information on your notepad. Start like this: *Do you think a ___ would make a good pet?* Be sure to change roles and then partners.

DON'T STOP!
• Make more suggestions.
• Describe the pros and cons of other pets.
• Say as much as you can.

RECYCLE THIS LANGUAGE
• attractive   • funny
• cute   • intelligent
• dangerous   • noisy
• disgusting   • patient
• energetic   • quiet
• fascinating   • ugly
• frightening

LESSON 3

GOAL Compare animal and human behavior

A ▶ 3:21 **LISTENING WARM-UP** VOCABULARY: ANIMAL SOCIAL GROUPS AND PROTECTIVE PHYSICAL FEATURES
Read and listen. Then listen again and repeat.

ANIMAL SOCIAL GROUPS

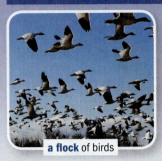
a flock of birds

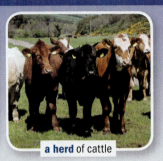
a herd of cattle

a school of fish

a pack of wolves

PHYSICAL FEATURES

claws

hooves (singular: a hoof)

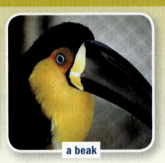
a beak

horns

B **APPLY NEW VOCABULARY** Complete the chart with a partner.

Animals with claws	Animals with hooves	Animals with horns

Birds with powerful beaks	Animals that travel in packs	Animals that gather in herds

C ▶ 3:22 **LISTEN TO DEFINE TERMS** Listen to Part 1 of the lecture to answer this question: What is the difference between an animal that is a predator and one that is prey?

D ▶ 3:23 **LISTEN FOR EXAMPLES** Listen to Part 1 of the lecture again. With a partner, find an example from the listening to explain each of the following:

1 a benefit of a social group for animals of prey ....
2 a benefit of a social group for predators ....
3 the role of a dominant animal in a social group ....
4 the meaning of "fight or flight" ....

E ▶ 3:24 **LISTEN FOR DETAILS** Now listen to Part 2 of the lecture and answer the questions.

1 What is the difference between learned behavior and instinct?
2 What are two examples of learned behavior from the lecture?

F **THINK AND EXPLAIN** Which of these situations do you think illustrate learned behavior as opposed to instinct? Explain your reasons, based on information from the lecture.

A

Hungry baby birds open their beaks wide so that an adult will put a worm inside.

B

Baby rabbits quickly follow their mother away from a potential predator.

C

Young cats respond to perceived danger by getting ready to run away or to fight.

G **APPLY IDEAS** Discuss the questions.

1 Look at the animals in Preview on page 62. Which are predators and which are prey? Which are both?
2 What are some ways in which you think humans behave: a) like herd animals or flocks or b) like animals who socialize in packs? Provide examples.

NOW YOU CAN Compare animal and human behavior

A **NOTEPADDING** In what ways do you think humans are the same as other animals? In what ways do you think we're completely different? Write some ideas.

How we're the same or similar	How we're very different
Groups provide safety and social interaction.	Humans are more able to respond to danger using their intelligence.

How we're the same or similar	How we're very different

B **DISCUSSION** Share your ideas with your classmates. Do you think we have more similarities to or differences from other animals? Use the examples from your notepad.

RECYCLE THIS LANGUAGE
- aggressive
- dangerous
- devoted
- in charge
- intelligent
- patient
- protective
- useful

LESSON 4 GOAL Debate the value of animal conservation

A READING WARM-UP What are some endangered animals you can think of? What are some threats to their survival?

B ▶ 3:25 READING Read the stories. What do you think ensured the survival of the buffalo in the U.S.?

The Will to Make a Difference

We live on a planet that is rich in biodiversity—there are millions of different species of animals and plants across the globe. Yet many species are disappearing at an alarming rate as the habitats in which plants and animals live together are reduced year after year. Currently, 11,000 species of plants and animals—including over 180 mammals—are at risk of becoming extinct because of this loss of habitat. Once gone, their disappearance is irreversible—they cannot be brought back. In its fast development as a nation over the last three hundred years, the United States has experienced some dramatic shifts in animal populations. Here is the story of a dismal failure and a remarkable success story.

an American bison

The Passenger Pigeon — FAILURE

Early European visitors to North America told amazing stories about huge flocks of passenger pigeons that darkened the sky for hours as they flew south for winter. They were easy targets for hunters, delicious to eat, and useful for making feather beds. Estimates put their total population at about five billion—the same number as the population of all birds combined in the U.S. today.

By the mid-1800s, the hunting of passenger pigeons had become a large-scale commercial enterprise, supplying east coast cities with a steady supply of birds. Around 300,000 a year were sent to New York City alone. At the same time, their habitat and food sources were shrinking as forests were cut down for farming and construction. In addition, approximately 250,000 birds were killed simply for sport each year. Making matters worse, a female passenger pigeon laid only one egg each year. By the turn of the twentieth century, any attempts to save the passenger pigeon were too late. The last surviving pigeon died in the Cincinnati Zoo in 1914—a species lost forever.

The American Bison (or Buffalo) — SUCCESS

Before European settlers came to North America, there were more than 50 million buffalo roaming in huge herds across the continent's central flatlands, which are today known as the Great Plains. These strange-looking, magnificent creatures—with their furry heads and shoulders and distinctive horns—were an important resource for food, clothing, and shelter for Native Americans living on the plains. And they played an enormous part in the plains ecosystem, sustaining other animals and plants. Weaker buffalo provided food for predators like bears and wolves. Herds attracted birds that picked at buffalo fur for insects. Thousands of hooves walking over the landscape prevented aggressive plants from taking over.

Buffalo hides were important in Native American life, including for shelter.

In the 1800s, as new settlers moved from the East to settle the West, whole herds were slaughtered, often just for sport. Buffalo were considered an obstacle to the settlers' desire to grow crops and raise cattle. The resource that sustained Native Americans for centuries began to disappear. By the end of the 1800s, there were as few as 750 buffalo remaining.

Many people were shocked that the buffalo, long considered a symbol of the West, had been allowed to come so close to extinction. Fortunately, efforts to save them were begun in 1905. The remaining herds were gathered together and protected. Their number steadily increased to today's population of about 350,000.

What conclusion can we draw from these stories?

In the case of the passenger pigeon, extinction was occurring so fast that, even with efforts to save them, it was too late to act. However, we can see that with the American buffalo, conservation efforts can make a difference if they are begun early enough.

C UNDERSTAND MEANING FROM CONTEXT   Choose the correct meaning for each word.

1 biodiversity
   a the place where animals live
   b the variety of living things
   c the disappearance of a species

2 a habitat
   a the food animals eat
   b the place animals live
   c the number of species

3 extinction
   a the protection of a species
   b the hunting of a species
   c the disappearance of a species

4 conservation
   a the protection of animals from extinction
   b a danger to animals
   c a source of food

5 an ecosystem
   a a danger to animals
   b the protection of a species
   c a community of living things

D RECOGNIZE CAUSE AND EFFECT   Discuss these questions with a partner.

1 What are four reasons the passenger pigeon became extinct? Why did conservation efforts fail?
2 Why did settlers hunt the buffalo? How did the buffalo come so close to extinction?

NOW YOU CAN   Debate the value of animal conservation

A FRAME YOUR IDEAS
With a partner, read and discuss the arguments for and against animal conservation. Which arguments are the strongest for each side of the animal conservation debate? Which are the weakest?

For	Against
• Human beings have a responsibility to protect all living things.	• Extinctions are simply part of the natural process—it's the principle of "survival of the fittest."
• Species should be preserved for future generations.	• Environmental protection costs a lot of money. It's "a luxury" for countries that have more serious problems.
• Natural parks that protect wildlife are big tourist attractions that generate jobs and income for local economies.	• Millions of species have already become extinct with no significant impact on the environment—it's no big deal.
• Species extinction is happening at such a fast rate we'd be foolish not to act quickly.	• Conservation limits land available to farmers, who really need it for their livelihood.
• For every species lost to extinction, humans miss the chance to make new discoveries—for example, new medicines.	• Do we really need 2,000 species of mice?
• Your own ideas: ………………………………	• Your own ideas: ………………………………

B DEBATE
Form two groups—one for and one against this statement: *It's important to protect all species of animals from extinction*. Take turns presenting and supporting your views with reasons and examples.

❝ I don't see why we should worry about conserving one type of endangered frog or salamander. There are many other kinds that are not endangered. ❞

❝ But the extinction of one type of frog could affect mammals and reptiles that may depend on that species for food. ❞

❝ Come to think of it, you have a point! ❞

RECYCLE THIS LANGUAGE
- amphibians
- birds
- fish
- invertebrates
- mammals
- reptiles

OPTIONAL WRITING
Write at least two paragraphs about the reasons some animals become endangered. Describe the threats to their survival and what can be done to save them.

WRITING Supporting a point of view

A WRITING SKILL   Study the rules.

To persuade readers to agree with your point of view in an essay:

- State your point of view in the introduction to your essay.
- Then provide examples, facts, or experts' opinions that support your point of view.
- Another effective technique is to demonstrate the weakness of opposing arguments.
- Summarize your main point in a concluding sentence.

Use expressions like these to support your point of view. Pay attention to correct punctuation when needed.

Support your point of view	Offer experts' opinions
For one thing,	[Smith] states that …
For example,	According to [Rivera], …
For instance,	Studies suggest that …
Furthermore,	

Refute opposing arguments	Conclude your argument
It can be argued that …	In conclusion,
[Some people] think … } However,	In summary,
It [may be] true that …	To sum up,

WRITING MODEL

Many people question whether it's humane to keep animals in zoos. However, **today's zoos can play an important role in animal conservation.** They can do this in a number of ways.

For one thing, studies suggest that animal conservation research and observation may be conducted more easily in zoos. In that way, new methods for ensuring the survival of endangered species might be discovered. **Furthermore,** in her report on conservation efforts at the Parkland Zoo, **biologist Ann Fisher states that** zoos can protect the young of endangered species until they are old enough to be released into the wild. **It can be argued that** all animals should be free and that it is unethical to keep any animals in zoos. **However,** the survival of these species in the wild may actually depend on the results of the scientific studies many zoos provide.

In conclusion, I believe endangered animals should be kept in zoos in order to support conservation efforts. It's one way that we can help ensure their survival.

B PRACTICE   Complete the arguments to support the point of view.

Zoos can play an increasingly important role in animal conservation. **1 (For one thing, / However,)** a zoo is a good environment for scientists to observe the behavior of endangered animals. Information from this research can be used to ensure their survival. **2 (Many people think / For example,)** animals are simply cooped up in cages at zoos. **3 (Furthermore, / However,)** today's modern zoos try to imitate their natural habitats by providing healthy food and lots of space for exercise and play. Without this intervention, many species would not survive in the wild. **4 (According to / To sum up)** Dutch scientist Frans de Wall, zoos also serve an important educational purpose. **5 (Furthermore, / For example,)** by visiting zoos with their families or school classes, children learn about endangered animals and grow up appreciating the importance of protecting them. **6 (To sum up, / It may be true that)** there are good reasons for keeping endangered animals in zoos.

C APPLY THE WRITING SKILL   Write a short essay in which you express your opinion on the treatment of animals on farms or in research. Use persuasion to get the reader to agree with your point of view. State your point of view in the introduction. Support it with examples, facts, or experts' opinions. Refute opposing arguments. Conclude by restating your main point.

OPTIONAL WRITING   Exchange paragraphs with a partner. Do you agree or disagree with your partner's point of view? Write a short response, explaining why. Start like this: *I [agree / disagree] with your argument because …*

SELF-CHECK

☐ Did I state my point of view clearly in the introduction?
☐ Did I provide examples, facts, or experts' opinions to support my point of view?
☐ Did I discuss opposing arguments?
☐ Did I include a concluding sentence?

REVIEW

A ▶ 3:26 Listen to Part 1 of a radio program. Choose the phrase that best completes each statement, according to the program.

1. Capuchin monkeys can be …… .
   a used for medical research   b loyal friends to humans   c trained to help people with disabilities
2. These monkeys are useful to humans because they …… .
   a can do simple jobs   b can push a wheelchair   c can wash dishes

B ▶ 3:27 Now listen to Part 2 and choose the phrase that best completes each statement.

1. Dolphin-assisted therapy had a positive effect on children's …… .
   a moral or ethical development   b speech development   c physical development
2. Children respond to dolphins because dolphins are …… .
   a good swimmers   b intelligent   c playful
3. Many of these children respond better to people after …… .
   a a year of treatment   b a few treatments   c a few weeks of treatment

C Change the adjective in each statement so it makes sense.

1. A relaxed pet that is good with kids is ~~destructive~~. ……………………
2. A cat that often scratches people with its claws is ~~affectionate~~. ……………………
3. A pet that is loving and friendly is ~~aggressive~~. ……………………
4. A dog that damages furniture is ~~playful~~. ……………………
5. An animal that is easy to care for is ~~filthy~~. ……………………
6. A dog that is easily frightened is ~~protective~~. ……………………
7. A pet that is expensive to buy and take care of is ~~good-natured~~. ……………………
8. A parrot that has fun holding a ball in its beak is ~~loyal~~. ……………………

D Complete each statement with vocabulary from the unit.

1. Passenger pigeons used to fly together in very large ………………… .
2. A cat is a mammal, and a frog is an ………………… .
3. Dogs that do not have owners sometimes hang out together in ………………… .
4. Lions use their teeth and ………………… to kill their prey.
5. Buffalo have a pair of ………………… on their furry heads.
6. An eel is a kind of fish, and a crocodile is a kind of ………………… .
7. Dominant male sheep fight with their horns to choose who will be the one in charge of the ………………… .
8. Humans have feet, and horses have ………………… .
9. A bird may use its ………………… to protect itself from a predator.

E Choose four of the topics. Use passive modals to state your own opinion about each topic.

Topics		
medical research	dog fighting	pets
hunting	extinction	zoos

Example: _Hunting should be banned because it is inhumane._

1 ……………………………………………………………………………………
2 ……………………………………………………………………………………
3 ……………………………………………………………………………………
4 ……………………………………………………………………………………

TEST-TAKING SKILLS BOOSTER   p. 156

Web Project: Treatment of Animals
www.english.com/summit3e

UNIT 7

Advertising and Consumers

COMMUNICATION GOALS
1. Evaluate ways and places to shop
2. Discuss your reactions to ads
3. Discuss problem shopping behavior
4. Persuade someone to buy a product

PREVIEW

A **FRAME YOUR IDEAS** Read four examples of shopping behavior and rate them.

READ ABOUT FOUR SHOPPING MISTAKES.

Number the mistakes in order of seriousness, from 1 to 4, with 4 being the most serious.

When I'm feeling blue, it cheers me up to go shopping and splurge on a few luxury items.

I may have gone a little overboard this time. But I just can't pass up a good sale, even if I don't need anything at the moment.

Everyone's buying it, so it must be terrific. I guess I'll buy it, too.

When I see a famous person I respect endorsing a product, then I know it's good.

B **DISCUSSION** In your opinion, what causes people to behave in the ways the people in the pictures do? In what way is their behavior similar? Do you know anyone like these people? Explain.

C ▶ 4:01 **SPOTLIGHT** Read and listen to a conversation between two colleagues. Notice the spotlighted language.

ENGLISH FOR TODAY'S WORLD
Understand a variety of accents.
Aldo = Italian
Sofia = Spanish

Aldo: Oh, no! **I could kick myself**!
Sofia: About what?
Aldo: You know how much I've been wanting to learn Spanish, right? Look at this great system I could have gotten for half price. Well, until yesterday, that is.
Sofia: Oh, come on. **Don't fall for that.** You can't learn a language while you sleep.
Aldo: I don't know. They say it's based on brain science. And it's risk-free. You get your money back if you don't learn. So it must be true.
Sofia: Oh, Aldo. **That's just wishful thinking.** Think about how long it took you to learn English.
Aldo: But **you're comparing apples and oranges.** Learning Spanish is a whole lot easier than learning English for Italian speakers like me.
Sofia: **That's debatable.** Not everyone would agree with that. But whatever. Any new language takes plenty of study and practice.
Aldo: I know. But I hate being forced to learn grammar. In this method I don't think you have to.
Sofia: Sorry. **There are no two ways about it.** Learning a language takes work … . **Tell you what.** I'll teach you Spanish myself! Between now and the end of the year, we'll have dinner together a couple of evenings a week. We'll converse in Spanish. You'll learn fast.
Aldo: You really mean it? I'd be willing to pay you for the lessons.
Sofia: No way. Just make me a nice Italian dinner on those nights, and **we'll call it even.** It'll be fun!
Aldo: Dinner? No problem! I'd be making that anyway… . Sofia, this is really generous of you.
Sofia: Well, you've done me a bunch of favors at work. I figure **I owe you one**!

RISK FREE! **Miracle Method**
Be fluent in Spanish in 6 weeks. Just listen while you sleep.
HURRY! Half-price offer ends November 15th.
Your money back if you can't speak Spanish by December 31st.

D **UNDERSTAND IDIOMS AND EXPRESSIONS** Write an expression from Spotlight with a similar meaning to each sentence below.

1 I'm going to suggest something to you. ....
2 You won't owe me anything. ....
3 These two things are completely different. ....
4 There is more than one opinion about that. ....
5 I regret something I did. ....
6 There's only one correct opinion about that. ....
7 Don't believe what they say. ....
8 You are hoping that it's true, but it isn't. ....
9 It's my turn to do something nice for you. ....

E **THINK AND EXPLAIN** With a partner, answer each question. Support your answers with specific information from Spotlight.

1 What is it about the ad that makes Aldo want to kick himself?
2 What does Sofia think of the Miracle Method?
3 What do you think Aldo hates about traditional language courses? Explain why.

SPEAKING **PAIR WORK** Discuss whether you think any of the people in the pictures on page 74 have anything in common with Aldo. Explain your reasons.

LESSON 1

GOAL Evaluate ways and places to shop

A ▶ 4:02 **VOCABULARY** **VERBS FOR SHOPPING ACTIVITIES** Read and listen to what the people are saying. Then listen and repeat.

browse take one's time looking at things without necessarily wanting to buy anything

comparison shop look at the prices of the same or similar items in order to decide which to buy

bargain hunt look around for things one can buy cheaply for less than their usual price

window shop look at things in store windows without going inside or intending to buy them

B ▶ 4:03 **LISTEN TO ACTIVATE VOCABULARY** Listen to the conversations about shopping. Infer what the people are doing. Complete each statement with the correct verb phrase.

1. The shoppers are (browsing / bargain hunting).
2. The people are (comparison shopping / window shopping).
3. The men are (window shopping / comparison shopping).
4. The woman is (window shopping / browsing).

76 UNIT 7

C PAIR WORK First, complete the chart. Then compare information with a partner.

Activity	When and why you do this activity
browsing	
bargain hunting	
window shopping	
comparison shopping	

> " I go window shopping when I have time on my hands and don't feel like spending money. "

NOW YOU CAN Evaluate ways and places to shop

A ▶ 4:04 **CONVERSATION SPOTLIGHT** Read and listen. Notice the spotlighted conversation strategies.

A: **Quick question.** Where would you go if you needed some new furniture?
B: Well, **I find** Morton's a good place to go bargain hunting.
A: Morton's? They can be a little pricey, can't they?
B: But when their things go on sale their prices are rock bottom.
A: **That's good to know.**
B: **Why don't you** check out Morton's online? Maybe you'll get lucky.

B ▶ 4:05 **RHYTHM AND INTONATION** Listen again and repeat. Then practice the conversation with a partner.

C NOTEPADDING Make a list of four places to shop, the best items to buy in each place, and the best shopping activities there.

place	items to buy there	ways to shop there
the public market	handicrafts and gifts	bargain hunt

	place	items to buy there	ways to shop there
1			
2			
3			
4			

D CONVERSATION ACTIVATOR
Create a conversation similar to the one in Ex. A, using information from your notepad. Start like this: *Quick question. Where …* Be sure to change roles and then partners.

DON'T STOP!
- Discuss other places for bargains.
- Ask for recommendations for places to buy other things.
- Suggest shopping together.
- Say as much as you can.

RECYCLE THIS LANGUAGE
- expensive
- cheap
- affordable
- pricey
- a bargain
- save money
- cost an arm and a leg
- rock bottom

LESSON 2

GOAL Discuss your reactions to ads

A ▶ 4:06 **GRAMMAR SPOTLIGHT** Read the interviews. Notice the spotlighted grammar.

What's the most annoying commercial or ad you've ever seen?

That would be the toothpaste ad they keep playing on my favorite music station. It's loud and obnoxious, and it totally gets on my nerves. I hate **to be forced** to listen to a dumb ad over and over. It just drives me crazy.

Nadia Basri, English teacher Amman, Jordan

What's the funniest ad you've ever seen?

There's this one really funny TV commercial for a language school. This cat sticks its claw into a goldfish bowl. Suddenly, the goldfish starts barking like an angry dog and the terrified cat runs away. The words "It never hurts to know another language" appear on the screen. It just cracks me up every time I see it. I enjoy **being entertained** like that.

Alex Winston, architect Pusan, South Korea

What's the most interesting ad you've ever seen?

An ad I saw yesterday really blew me away. There's this company that produces sports drinks. Their ad presents actual statistics of how the drink enhances athletic performance. It was so convincing I totally forgot it was an ad! Like most people, I resent simply **being sold to** and really appreciate **being informed** about a product's benefits. Ads like that can really build goodwill for a product.

Theresa Selden, advertising executive Minneapolis, USA

What's the most touching ad you've ever seen?

Actually, there's a billboard for a tablet that I see on my way to work. It shows this elderly woman having a video chat with her daughter and brand-new granddaughter. The tablet and the video chat are obviously something really new for the grandma. I'm not an emotional guy, but this ad just hits me in the heart and chokes me up. I know it's just an ad, but once in a while it doesn't hurt **to be reminded** about the important things in life.

Marcos Teixeira, medical student Fortaleza, Brazil

B UNDERSTAND MEANING FROM CONTEXT   Match the expressions with their meaning.

.... 1 It blows me away.
.... 2 It gets on my nerves.
.... 3 It cracks me up.
.... 4 It chokes me up.

a It makes me feel like crying.
b It annoys me.
c It amazes me.
d It makes me want to laugh.

Remember:
- Some verbs are followed by gerunds, some by infinitives, and some by either.
- Certain adjectives are often followed by infinitives.
- Certain expressions are followed by gerunds.

See pages 123–124 for a complete list.

C GRAMMAR   PASSIVE FORMS OF GERUNDS AND INFINITIVES

Use the passive form of a gerund (being + a past participle) or an infinitive (to be + a past participle) to focus on an action instead of on who performed the action.

Gerunds: affirmative and negative
I don't like **being forced** to watch commercials.
Susan hates **not being told** the truth.

Infinitives: affirmative and negative
We would like **to be called** when it goes on sale.
They were angry **not to be told** about the meeting.

Questions
Do you enjoy **being entertained** by commercials on TV?
Don't you resent **being required** to watch ads in movie theaters?
Doesn't your sister want **to be called** by her first name?
Who likes **being shown** commercials every few minutes?
Where do you like **being seated** in a restaurant?

GRAMMAR BOOSTER p. 136
The passive voice: review and expansion

D GRAMMAR PRACTICE Complete the conversations with passive gerunds or infinitives.

1. **A:** I think people enjoy (informed) ………………………… about new products.
   B: True, but I don't want (treat) ………………………… as if I don't know anything. Advertisers sometimes make me feel that way.

2. **A:** I don't like (show) ………………………… pictures of suffering animals in ads for animal charities. They're just too upsetting.
   B: I agree. I'm happy (ask) ………………………… to contribute just based on the facts. I don't need (show) ………………………… pictures.

3. **A:** This midnight sale is going to be great. Don't you love (give) ………………………… a chance to get everything at half-price?
   B: Actually, I'm annoyed at (force) ………………………… to wait in line all day and evening just to get in.

4. **A:** When I read an ad in a magazine, I would like (tell) ………………………… the whole truth, not half-truths.
   B: I know how you feel. I expect (treat) ………………………… with respect.

5. **A:** Companies want their products (advertise) ………………………… on TV during prime time—when the most people are watching.
   B: Maybe that's why advertisers complain about (charge) ………………………… so much for every minute they buy. They say that's why the products are so expensive.

> **PRONUNCIATION BOOSTER** p. 146
> Vowel sounds /i/ and /ɪ/

E GRAMMAR PRACTICE Rewrite each sentence, using a passive gerund or infinitive to replace the underlined words. Don't use a <u>by</u> phrase.

Example: I don't mind <u>when advertisers inform me</u> about new products.

> I don't mind being informed about new products.

1. I can't stand <u>advertisers' forcing me</u> to watch ads over and over again.
2. I resent <u>one company's telling me</u> that I shouldn't buy another company's product.
3. We can't tolerate <u>telemarketers' calling us</u> while we're eating dinner.

Types of ads
- TV commercials
- pop-up ads on websites
- radio ads
- magazine or newspaper ads
- billboards on highways and buildings
- other online ads

NOW YOU CAN Discuss your reactions to ads

A FRAME YOUR IDEAS Complete the chart with ads you are familiar with.

	Name or type of product	Type of ad
An ad that's interesting		
An ad that cracks me up		
An ad that gets on my nerves		
An ad that blows me away		
An ad that chokes me up		
An ad that drives me crazy		

B DISCUSSION ACTIVATOR Describe and compare the ads on your chart. Use passive forms of gerunds and infinitives. Say as much as you can.

> 66 There's a TV commercial for shampoo that really gets on my nerves. I'm sick of being forced to watch it over and over! 99

Describing how you feel
- I like …
- I appreciate …
- I love …
- I enjoy …
- I hate …
- I prefer …
- I need …
- I don't like …
- I don't appreciate …
- I can't stand …
- I dislike …
- I resent …
- I miss …
- I want …

LESSON 3 **GOAL** Discuss problem shopping behavior

A **READING WARM-UP** Are you a careful shopper? Or do you lack self-control when you shop?

  B ▶ 4:07 **READING** Read the article. In what ways is compulsive shopping a problem?

COMPULSIVE SHOPPING: An addiction or just something to get under control?

For some people, shopping is a favorite pastime and harmless, as long as they have the money to pay for their purchases. For others, unfortunately, shopping can spiral out of control and become as serious as other destructive addictions like alcoholism, drug abuse, and compulsive gambling.

Research has shown that compulsive shopping, like other addictions, causes the physical effect of a "high," when brain chemicals such as endorphins and dopamine are released. This causes the addict to feel pleasurable sensations. These sensations make shopping hard to resist, and thus the habit hard to kick. What are the warning signs of a shopping addiction, or as it is sometimes called, "shopaholism"?

First, just as alcoholics tend to hide their bottles, shopaholics commonly hide their purchases. Shopaholics often lie to people in their families about how much money they've spent.

Second, the problem is long-lived, or "chronic," meaning that the behavior doesn't occur just once or twice a year. Rather, it's a continuous problem that repeats itself over and over.

Third, shopaholics, like many people, purchase items on impulse. But unlike normal people who sometimes splurge and pick up an impulse item like a sweater they don't need, shopaholics might buy ten.

Fourth, as with any addiction, a problem exists when the behavior has obvious consequences: going into debt, going shopping instead of taking care of family or work responsibilities, or uncontrollable spending that may deprive others in the family of money needed for other things.

What can true shopaholics do to get help? For some, self-help and group programs can be effective. For others, whose addiction results from underlying depression, seeing a psychotherapist or a physician can help, reducing the need to shop compulsively.

Thankfully, many people are able to splurge or buy things on impulse from time to time without being addicts. However, if you are concerned you may be a compulsive shopper, here are some tips that can help.

- Shop with a list. It keeps you focused on the things you really need and want. And it ensures that you don't get distracted by impulse items and go overboard, buying a lot of unneeded things.

- Avoid sales, coupons, and special offers. Spending any money on something you don't need is overspending, even if it's a bargain. Remember: Special offers are a way for store owners to get you into the store.

- Follow the "thinking time" rule: Don't buy anything new on the spot. Make yourself wait a day, a week, or some other amount of time before making a purchase. Or do some comparison-shopping. You may find you don't want the item after all, or you may find it at a much better price.

- Always try to be aware of your motivations when you shop. Don't go shopping when you're angry or upset. In the long run, the problem that upset you in the first place will still be there.

C **UNDERSTAND MEANING FROM CONTEXT** Find each of these words and phrases in the article. With a partner, discuss what they mean and write a sentence using each one.

1 an addiction
2 get something under control
3 a high
4 hard to kick
5 a shopaholic
6 chronic
7 splurge
8 go overboard
9 on the spot

D IDENTIFY SUPPORTING DETAILS Answer the questions, providing details from the article to support your answer.

1 In what ways is compulsive shopping like other addictions? Be specific.
2 Why are addictions so hard to overcome?
3 What are some consequences of shopaholism?
4 What is one possible cause for compulsive shopping in some people?
5 In what way is going overboard occasionally different from a true shopping addiction?

NOW YOU CAN Discuss problem shopping behavior

A FRAME YOUR IDEAS Check the statements that are true for you.

What kind of SHOPPER are you?

Everyone goes a little overboard shopping from time to time. Take the survey to determine if your shopping is out of control.

- I could sometimes kick myself for how I spend my money.
- When I go shopping, I can't resist the temptation to buy something—I just can't come home empty-handed.
- I feel uncomfortable if I haven't bought anything in a week.
- I go shopping for an item I need, but I lose control and come home with a lot of things I don't need.
- I spend more than I should in order to get more expensive designer names and labels.
- I can't pass up a good sale. Even if I don't need anything, I just have to indulge myself and buy something.
- I sometimes lie to people about how much my purchases cost.
- I get more pleasure out of spending money than saving money.
- I don't have the patience to wait a day before buying something. If I want it, I buy it on the spot.

TOTAL THE NUMBER OF BOXES YOU CHECKED. IF YOUR TOTAL IS:

0–3 Great! Keep up the good habits!

4–5 Not too bad! Congratulations for admitting you're not perfect!

6–7 Uh-oh! Sounds like trouble may be around the corner!

8–9 Red alert! It's time to take the bull by the horns and change some of the ways you shop and spend money.

B DISCUSSION Choose one of the topics and meet in small groups with other classmates who have chosen the same topic. Share your conclusions with the class.

1 Do you think most people tend to go a little overboard with their shopping? Explain.
2 Do you think people should spend money only on things they need and never on things they don't need? Is it OK to buy on impulse sometimes?

RECYCLE THIS LANGUAGE
- That's debatable.
- You're comparing apples and oranges.
- There are no two ways about it.
- That's just wishful thinking.
- You really mean it?
- Whatever.

OPTIONAL WRITING Write a brochure offering help or advice for people with problem shopping behavior. Include a list of tips.

GOAL Persuade someone to buy a product

A LISTENING WARM-UP
PAIR WORK Read about eight advertising techniques used to persuade people to buy products. With a partner, discuss the techniques and write the letter of the example that illustrates each technique.

8 Eight techniques used by SUCCESSFUL ADVERTISERS

1 PROVIDE FACTS AND FIGURES
Prove the superiority of a product with statistics and objective, factual information.

2 CONVINCE PEOPLE TO "JUMP ON THE BANDWAGON"
Imply that *everyone* is using a product, and that others should too, in order to be part of the group.

3 PLAY ON PEOPLE'S HIDDEN FEARS
Imply that a product will protect the user from some danger or an uncomfortable situation.

4 PLAY ON PEOPLE'S PATRIOTISM
Imply that buying a product shows love of one's country.

5 PROVIDE "SNOB APPEAL"
Imply that use of a product makes the customer part of an elite group.

6 ASSOCIATE POSITIVE QUALITIES WITH A PRODUCT
Promote a product with words and ideas having positive meanings and associations.

7 PROVIDE TESTIMONIALS
Use a famous person or an "average consumer" to endorse a product so the consumer wants it too.

8 MANIPULATE PEOPLE'S EMOTIONS
Use images to appeal to customers' feelings, such as love, anger, or sympathy.

Examples

a A professional soccer player recommends a particular brand of shirts.

b A hotel chain shows a businesswoman in her room, calling home to talk to her children.

c A soft drink manufacturer shows young people having a great time drinking its product at the beach.

d A car manufacturer states how quickly its car can go from 0 to 100 kilometers per hour.

e A coffee manufacturer shows people dressed in formal attire drinking its brand of coffee at an art exhibition.

f A credit card company claims that its card is used by more people than any other card.

g A clothing manufacturer promotes its clothes by saying they are made by and for people in this country.

h An educational toy company suggests that other children will do better in school than yours will if you don't buy its toy today.

B ▶ 4:08 VOCABULARY WAYS TO PERSUADE
Listen and repeat. Then, based on the way they are used in Exercise A, write the correct word for each definition.

endorse
promote
imply
prove

1 personally recommend a product in exchange for payment: ....
2 show that something is definitely true, especially by providing facts, information, etc.: ....
3 suggest that something is true, without saying or showing it directly: ....
4 make sure people know about a new product in order to persuade them to buy it: ....

C ▶ 4:09 **LISTEN TO INFER** Listen to each ad. Write two techniques from Exercise A that the advertiser uses in the ad. Then listen again and take notes of what the ad says to support your choice of techniques.

Ad 1

Techniques used
....
....
....

Supporting details
....
....
....
....

Ad 2

Techniques used
....
....
....

Supporting details
....
....
....
....

Ad 3

Techniques used
....
....
....

Supporting details
....
....
....
....

D **APPLY IDEAS** With a partner, discuss some ads you know and decide which techniques they use.

NOW YOU CAN Persuade someone to buy a product

A **NOTEPADDING** In a group, choose a product and create a magazine, newspaper, Internet pop-up, or radio advertisement for it. Use one or more advertising techniques to persuade your classmates to buy the product. Make notes.

Ideas
- a car
- an airline
- a drink
- a smart phone
- a language school
- a brand of toothpaste
- your own idea: _____

Plan your ad
Type of product:
Name of product:
Type of ad:
Technique(s):

B **PRESENTATION** Present your ad to your class. Show it, read it, or act it out. Analyze your classmates' ads and discuss which techniques were used. As a class, assign awards for these categories:

- the funniest ad
- the most annoying ad
- the most persuasive ad
- the most interesting ad
- the most touching ad

83

WRITING: Summarize and paraphrase someone's point of view

A WRITING SKILL Study the rules.

A summary is a shortened explanation of the main ideas of an article. When writing a summary, include only the author's main points, not your own reactions or opinions. In your summary, be sure to paraphrase what the author said, putting the main idea into your own words.

Use a variety of reporting verbs to paraphrase the writer's ideas:

The report **argues** that …
Doctors **believe** that …
Experts **explain** that …
The article **states** that …
The writer **points out** that …
The journalist **reports** that …
The author **concludes** that …

Some other common expressions for reporting another person's ideas:

According to [Smith], …
In [the writer's] **opinion**, …
As [the article explains], …
From [García's] **point of view**, …

MODEL

The original text: "For some people, shopping is a favorite pastime and harmless, as long as they have the money to pay for their purchases. For others, unfortunately, shopping can spiral out of control and become as serious as other destructive addictions like alcoholism, drug abuse, and compulsive gambling."

Your summary and paraphrase: The author points out that shopping can be harmless for some but a serious addiction for others.

B PRACTICE Paraphrase these sentences from the article on page 80.

1 "Research has shown that compulsive shopping, like other addictions, causes the physical effects of a "high," when brain chemicals, such as endorphins and dopamine, are released."

....

2 "For others, unfortunately, shopping can spiral out of control and become as serious as other destructive addictions like alcoholism, drug abuse, and compulsive gambling."

....

C PRACTICE Reread the paragraphs that begin with *First*, *Second*, *Third*, and *Fourth* in the article on page 80. Then, in your own words, state the main idea of each paragraph, using reporting verbs and expressions suggested in Exercise A Writing Skill.

First
Second
Third
Fourth

D APPLY THE WRITING SKILL Write a summary of the article on page 80 by combining the main ideas from your notepad. Be sure to paraphrase what the author says, using your own words. Your summary should be no more than four to six sentences long.

SELF-CHECK
☐ Does the summary include only the author's main ideas?
☐ Did I paraphrase the author's ideas?
☐ Was I careful not to include my opinion in the summary?

OPTIONAL WRITING Write a short article in which you suggest how to avoid compulsive shopping.

REVIEW

A ▶ 4:10 Listen to each statement or question. Choose an appropriate response.

1. a There are no two ways about it.
   b They're comparing apples and oranges.
2. a Thanks! I owe you one.
   b That's just wishful thinking.
3. a Don't worry. We'll call it even.
   b That's debatable.
4. a Don't fall for that.
   b There are just no two ways about it.
5. a I know. I could kick myself!
   b Tell you what.

B On a separate sheet of paper, answer the questions.

1. What always cracks you up about your favorite TV comedy or movie?
2. Whose music blows you away?
3. What songs choke you up?
4. What gets on your nerves about public transportation?

C Complete the statements with passive forms of gerunds or infinitives.

1. I don't recall .... any information.
   send
2. They want .... more time for the project.
   give
3. She arranged .... to the airport.
   take
4. I was disappointed .... the news.
   tell
5. He risked .... from his job.
   fire
6. We were delighted .... to the wedding.
   invite

D On a separate sheet of paper, answer the questions in your own way.

1. What kinds of things do you like to splurge on?
2. Have you ever gone a little overboard when you were shopping? Explain.
3. What can't you resist the temptation to do? Why?

E Complete each statement with the correct form of one of the verbs.

| promote | endorse | prove | imply |

1. I'm sure Shiny Teeth toothpaste is the best. After all, it's being .... by that British actor with the gorgeous teeth. What's his name again?
2. This month Banana computers is .... a new laptop. It's smaller than a tablet and bigger than a smart phone, but it has full computer functionality.
3. Well, they don't have the statistics to .... that their shampoo grows hair, but all the pictures and testimonials .... that it probably will.

TEST-TAKING SKILLS BOOSTER p. 157

Web Project: Advertising Techniques
www.english.com/summit3e

UNIT 8

Family Trends

COMMUNICATION GOALS
1. Describe family trends
2. Discuss parent-teen issues
3. Compare generations
4. Discuss caring for the elderly

PREVIEW

A FRAME YOUR IDEAS Fill out the opinion survey of your attitudes about parent-teen relationships.

Check the opinion in each pair that YOU agree with more.

1. Teens should have to help around the house. It helps them develop a sense of responsibility.

   Teens shouldn't have to help around the house. They already have enough to do with their schoolwork.

2. Parents should buy things that teens demand in order to "keep the peace."

   Teens shouldn't always get everything they ask for. It would be a bad lesson for life.

3. Parents should set curfews. Teens who stay out late are likely to get in trouble.

   Teenagers shouldn't have curfews. They should be able to decide what time to come home.

4. Parents should make rules for teen behavior so teens learn right from wrong.

   Teens need to learn by making their own mistakes.

5. Parents should always ground teens if they misbehave. If they can't go out with their friends, they'll stop misbehaving and won't become troublemakers.

   Teens who don't obey the rules should be given a second chance before being grounded.

6. Parents should control what their teenage children do on the Internet. It's their job to protect their children from danger.

   Teenagers have a right to privacy, and their parents ought to respect it. What teens do on the Internet should be off-limits to parents.

B PAIR WORK Compare your opinions on the survey with a partner. Support your opinions with reasons.

" Parents don't have the right to know everything their kids do on the Internet. It isn't possible, anyway, because kids can delete their online history if they don't want their parents to see what they're doing. "

" I think that depends on the age of the kid. "

C ▶ 4:11 **SPOTLIGHT** Read and listen to a conversation about relationships. Notice the spotlighted language.

> **ENGLISH** FOR TODAY'S WORLD
> Understand a variety of accents.
> Grace = American English (standard)
> Margot = French

Grace: Did you hear the good news? Emma and Max **patched things up**!
Margot: They got back together? I didn't even know they'**d split up**! Shows you how out of touch I am. What happened?
Grace: Well, from what I understand, first they **had a falling out** about money, and then one thing led to another, and the marriage started **going downhill**.
Margot: What a shame. It's incredible how little things can snowball…. You know what, though? There's usually some bigger underlying issue when a marriage gets into trouble.
Grace: Actually, I think you'**ve hit the nail on the head**. Emma's been making more money than Max for the last couple of years, and then about six months ago he lost his job. So they figured it would be economical for him be a stay-at-home dad. I mean, why pay a babysitter?
Margot: Makes sense.
Grace: But that's just about the time things began to **fall apart**, and they started arguing about who should make financial decisions. And then the more they fought, the worse things got. Apparently, the constant conflict affected the kids' behavior. They just stopped obeying family rules and started texting friends and playing on their phones during dinner—you know what kids do these days…
Margot: You know, I'm feeling sort of like a gossip talking about them **behind their backs**. Let's just be thankful they're back together now.

D **UNDERSTAND IDIOMS AND EXPRESSIONS** Choose the word or phrase with the same meaning.

1 It's hard to patch things up after a breakup.
 a repair a relationship
 b have financial problems
 c get a divorce

2 I didn't realize they'd split up.
 a separated
 b gotten back together
 c gotten out of touch

3 Lyn and Ed had a falling out about the children.
 a argued
 b agreed not to talk
 c made strict rules

4 Our relationship started going downhill last year.
 a improving
 b getting worse
 c getting back together

5 Anne hit the nail on the head when she figured out the underlying problem.
 a realized what the real reason was
 b became violent
 c made a lot of money

6 A husband and wife should discuss their problems before things start to fall apart.
 a get bad
 b get interesting
 c get better

7 When you talk about people behind their backs, you are a gossip.
 a so they know what you think about them
 b so they don't know what you say about them
 c so they're thankful

E **THINK AND EXPLAIN** Answer the questions with a partner. Then discuss with the class.

1 What is your opinion of the decision to have Max stay home to care for the kids?
2 Why do you think some couples get back together after breaking up?

SPEAKING **GROUP WORK** Tell your classmates about a time you or someone you know…

- had a difference of opinion with a parent or child
- had a falling out with a friend, relative, or colleague

Provide specific examples and use language from Spotlight and Preview if possible.

LESSON 1 GOAL Describe family trends

A ▶ 4:12 **GRAMMAR SPOTLIGHT** Read the information in the article. Notice the spotlighted grammar.

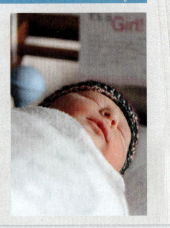

Today's News   January 22

FALLING BIRTHRATES

Current trends show the size of families is changing, impacting societies worldwide. Women are marrying later, and couples are waiting longer to have children. And **the longer** couples wait to have children, **the fewer** children they have.

Two key factors that impact family size are the education and the employment of women. Studies show that **the more** education women get, **the smaller** families they have. Moreover, **the longer** women stay in school, **the better** their opportunities for employment. Working women are less likely to marry young and have large families.

In addition to the falling birthrate, there is a rising life expectancy. With people living **longer and longer**, families are going to have to face the challenges posed by an aging population. **The longer** people live, **the more** care they require. Traditionally, children have cared for their elderly parents at home. However, **the more** the birthrate falls, **the harder** the future may be for the elderly. With fewer children, families may find it **more and more** difficult to care for their older members.

B **PAIR WORK** Discuss the questions.

1 According to the article, what factors explain why more couples are having fewer children?
2 Why do you think populations are living longer? What problems can be caused by a larger elderly population?

C **GRAMMAR** REPEATED COMPARATIVES AND DOUBLE COMPARATIVES

Repeated comparatives
Use repeated comparatives to describe continuing increases and decreases.
   The birthrate is getting **lower and lower**.
   By the end of the twentieth century, couples were waiting **longer and longer** to marry.
   Changes are occurring **faster and faster**.

Use repeated comparatives with <u>more</u> or <u>less</u> to modify adjectives or adverbs that don't use an -er comparative form. When the adjective or adverb is understood, it may be omitted.
   It's becoming **more and more difficult** to predict life expectancy.
   It's **less and less possible** to raise birthrates in modern societies.
   That's happening **more and more** (often) these days.

Use repeated comparatives with <u>more</u>, <u>less</u>, and <u>fewer</u> to compare nouns. When the noun is understood, it may be omitted.
   More and more people are marrying later.
   Fewer and fewer (people) are having children before they are thirty.

Double comparatives
Use double comparatives to describe a cause-and-effect process.
   The more education women get, **the later** they marry. [Women are getting more education, so they're marrying later.]
   The less children studied, **the more** slowly they learned. [Children studied less, so they learned more slowly.]
   The older one gets, **the harder** it can be to find a husband or wife.

Note: When <u>be</u> is used in double comparatives, it is sometimes omitted.
   The better the quality of health care (is), **the higher** the life expectancy (is).

> **GRAMMAR BOOSTER** p. 137
> • Making comparisons: review and expansion
> • Other uses of comparatives, superlatives, and comparisons with <u>as ... as</u>

> **Be careful!**
> Don't use the present or past continuous in either clause of a double comparative statement. Use the simple present or the simple past tense instead.
>   The longer couples **wait** to have children, the fewer children they **have**.
>   NOT The longer couples ~~are waiting~~ to have children, the fewer they~~'re having~~.

88 UNIT 8

D NOTICE THE GRAMMAR Find a sentence using a double comparative in Spotlight on page 87.

E ▶ 4:13 LISTEN TO ACTIVATE GRAMMAR Listen to three people talking about trends in marriage and family life. Then listen again and complete each statement, according to what the speaker implies, using double comparatives.

1 .... education mothers get, ... medical care they receive.
2 .... couples date, ... they marry.
3 .... children stay in school, ... their life expectancy.

F GRAMMAR PAIR WORK First complete the statements logically, using the cues and double comparatives. Then, with a partner, discuss whether you agree or disagree with each statement. Support your opinion.

1 .... people are when they marry, ... children they have.
    old   *few*
2 .... the life expectancy, ... the elderly population is.
    high   *large*
3 .... people work, ... they are.
    hard   *successful*
4 .... the quality of health care is, ... the death rate.
    good   *low*
5 .... the country is, ... the life expectancy.
    developed   *low*
6 .... women are when they have children, ... they are to get
    young   *likely*
a higher education.

G GRAMMAR PRACTICE On a separate sheet of paper, rewrite the sentences, using repeated comparative forms.

1 (An increasing number of) couples are having (a decreasing number of) children.
2 Divorces are taking place (with decreasing frequency).
3 People say that children are growing up (with increasing speed).

H GRAMMAR PRACTICE Correct the errors in the sentences.

1 The more I'm eating, the later I'm sleeping.
2 The fewer grammar mistakes I'm making when I speak English, the better I am communicating.

NOW YOU CAN Describe family trends

A PAIR WORK With a partner, take turns making statements with repeated and double comparatives about the way families are changing in your country.

> *Families have been getting smaller and smaller.*

B SUMMARIZE On a separate sheet of paper, write a paragraph developing one of the statements you made in Exercise A. Add details.

> *In the last few decades, family size has declined. Fewer and fewer people are having big families, so their standard of living is higher. The higher the standard of living is, the healthier the population will be.*

C DISCUSSION ACTIVATOR In small groups, discuss family trends in your country. Talk about how changing trends will impact the families of the future. Include the ideas below in your discussion. Say as much as you can.

Ideas
- birthrate
- life expectancy
- age at marriage
- health
- education
- income
- employment opportunities
- generational differences

> *It seems like more and more people are having fewer and fewer children. This could be a problem later because ...*

LESSON 2

GOAL Discuss parent-teen issues

A ▶ 4:14 **VOCABULARY** DESCRIBING PARENT AND TEEN BEHAVIOR
Read and listen. Then listen again and repeat.

Parents can sometimes be ...

(too) strict
They set a lot of restrictions and expect kids to obey rules.

(too) lenient
They let their kids have or do anything they want.

overprotective
They worry too much about their kids.

Teenagers can sometimes be ...

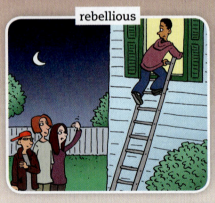
rebellious
They refuse to obey family rules and just do whatever they want.

spoiled
They expect to have or get whatever they want.

disrespectful
They are rude and often talk back to adults.

B **VOCABULARY PRACTICE** Complete each statement with one of the adjectives. Use <u>too</u> with the adjective if that represents your opinion.

1. Parents who always allow their teenage children to stay out late are ....
2. Teenagers who demand that their parents buy everything they ask for are ....
3. When parents never let their children do things because they are afraid they'll get sick or hurt, they are being ....
4. If a father tells his teenage son not to get a tattoo and he disobeys and gets one anyway, we say he is ....
5. Parents who make their teenage children clean their rooms every day are ....
6. Teens who act uninterested in class are ....

C ▶4:15 **LISTEN TO ACTIVATE VOCABULARY** Listen to the conversations about parent and teen behavior. Then listen again and determine which adjective from the Vocabulary best completes each statement.

1 She thinks he's ....
2 She thinks he's acting ....
3 He thinks she's ....
4 He's angry because she's being ....
5 He thinks she's ....
6 She criticizes him for being ....

D **MAKE PERSONAL COMPARISONS** Are you or anyone you know like any of the speakers in the conversations in Exercise C? Explain.

E **PROVIDE EXAMPLES** With a partner, describe people you know who exhibit the following kinds of behavior. Explain, providing real details.

1 a parent who is too strict
2 a parent who is too lenient
3 a parent who is overprotective
4 a teenager who is rebellious
5 a teenager who is spoiled
6 a teenager who is disrespectful

NOW YOU CAN Discuss parent-teen issues

A ▶4:16 **CONVERSATION SPOTLIGHT**
Read and listen. Notice the spotlighted conversation strategies.

A: What do you think parents should do if their teenage kids start smoking?
B: Well, I'm sorry to say there's not much they can do.
A: Why's that?
B: Well, teenagers are out of the house most of the day, so parents can't control everything they do.
A: I suppose. But they can ground them if they don't shape up.

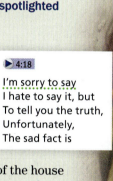
▶4:18
I'm sorry to say
I hate to say it, but
To tell you the truth,
Unfortunately,
The sad fact is

B ▶4:17 **RHYTHM AND INTONATION**
Listen again and repeat. Then practice the conversation with a partner.

C **CONVERSATION ACTIVATOR**
Create a similar conversation. Use the Vocabulary, examples of bad behavior from the list, and language from Preview on page 86. Start like this: *What do you think parents [or teenagers] should do if…?* Be sure to change roles and then partners.

DON'T STOP!
• Give examples of your own experiences.
• Discuss other parent-teen issues.
• Say as much as you can.

Examples of bad behavior
• acting up at school
• staying out late without permission
• being rude or disrespectful
• becoming a troublemaker
• another example: ....

D **DISCUSSION** If you could give parents one piece of advice, what would it be? If you could give teenagers one piece of advice, what would it be? Provide reasons.

91

LESSON 3
GOAL Compare generations

A ▶ 4:19 LISTENING WARM-UP WORD STUDY TRANSFORMING VERBS AND ADJECTIVES INTO NOUNS
Listen and repeat.

Noun Suffixes	Nouns		Noun Suffixes	Nouns	
-ation -tion -ssion	expect → explain → frustrate → permit →	expectation explanation frustration permission	-ness	fair → rebellious → selfish → strict →	fairness rebelliousness selfishness strictness
-ment	develop → involve →	development involvement	-ity	generous → mature → mobile → secure → productive →	generosity maturity mobility security productivity
-y	courteous → difficult →	courtesy difficulty			
-ility	responsible → reliable → capable → dependable → disabled →	responsibility reliability capability dependability disability	-ance -ence	important → significant → independent → lenient → obedient →	importance significance independence lenience obedience

B WORD STUDY PRACTICE Circle all the words that are nouns.
Check a dictionary if you are not sure about the meaning of a word.

1 dependency   depend   dependence   dependent
2 confidence   confident   confide   confidently
3 consider   consideration considerate   considerately
4 different   difference   differentiate   differentiation
5 attraction   attract   attractive   attractiveness
6 impatient   impatience   impatiently
7 unfair   unfairness   unfairly
8 closeness   close   closely
9 happily   happy   happiness

> **PRONUNCIATION BOOSTER** p. 147
> Stress placement: prefixes and suffixes

C ▶ 4:20 LISTEN FOR SUPPORTING INFORMATION
Listen to Part 1 of a man's description of the generation gap in his family. Then answer the questions.

1 How did Rimas grow up differently from his parents?
2 Why does Rimas's father think teenagers nowadays have more problems than when he was growing up?

D ▶ 4:21 LISTEN FOR DETAILS Listen to Part 1 again. Then complete each statement.

1 Rimas grew up in ...., but his parents grew up in ....
2 Rimas's extended family includes .... aunts and uncles on his mother's side.
3 When Rimas's mother was growing up, every evening she ate dinner .... However, when Rimas and his sister were kids, they sometimes had to eat ....

Rimas Vilkas
Vilnius, Lithuania

E ▶ 4:22 **LISTEN TO COMPARE AND CONTRAST** Now listen to Part 2. Then listen again and complete the chart by describing the differences between the two generations. Compare charts with a partner.

	How are they different?	
	Rimas's parents' generation	Rimas's generation
career choices		
mobility		
influences from other cultures		
age at marriage and childbearing		
work experience		
closeness of family		

F **RELATE TO PERSONAL EXPERIENCE** Discuss the questions.
1 Rimas's parents worry about him and their own future. From your experience, why do you think parents worry about their children and the future?
2 In what ways is the Vilkas family's story story similar to or different from yours?

NOW YOU CAN Compare generations

A **NOTEPADDING** Compare your parents' generation with your generation. Write your ideas. Discuss them with a partner.

	My parents' generation	My generation
music		
style of clothes		
hairstyles / facial hair		
attitude toward elders		
family responsibility		
language (idioms, slang)		
marriage and childbearing		
values and beliefs		
use of technology		
other:		

B **DISCUSSION** Discuss these questions with your classmates. Use information from your notepads for examples.
1 In what ways is your generation the most different from your parents' generation? What do you like best or respect the most about your parents' generation?
2 What contributions do you think your generation will make to the next generation? How do you think the next generation will differ from yours?

OPTIONAL WRITING Summarize your discussion in writing.

LESSON 4
GOAL Discuss caring for the elderly

A **READING WARM-UP** In your country, how are older family members traditionally cared for?

B ▶ 4:23 **READING** Read the report on the increase in the global population of older people. What will some consequences of this demographic shift be?

WORLDWIDE GROWTH OF AGING POPULATIONS

The world is facing a huge demographic shift without precedent. For the first time in history, we soon will have more elderly people than children, and more extremely old people than ever before. As the population of older people gets larger and larger, key questions arise: will aging be accompanied by a longer period of good health, social engagement, and productivity, or will it be associated with more illness, disability, and dependency?

What we do know is that the more elderly people there are in the population, the more cases of age-related diseases such as heart disease, stroke, diabetes, and cancer there will be. Societies will have to find ways to address this growing need. And the older people get, the higher the prevalence of dementia, especially Alzheimer's disease; an estimated 25–30 percent of people aged 85 or older have dementia and lose their ability to remember, have difficulty reasoning, and undergo some personality changes.

Unless new and more effective ways to treat or prevent Alzheimer's disease are found, cases are expected to rise dramatically with the increased aging of the population worldwide. And because most dementia patients eventually need constant care and help with the most basic activities of daily living, more institutions will need to be built for their care, more medications provided for their treatment, and more caregivers trained to aid them in their daily life.

What are some of the other social and economic consequences of this demographic shift? Even if they don't have dementia,

SALVADOR DUARTE is in rehabilitation to learn to walk after a stroke. In the coming decades more and more elderly patients like Mr. Duarte will require costly rehabilitation.

ELEANOR HARRIS (left) lived on her own until last year, when her daughter found her in the kitchen cooking what she thought was soup, but which was actually just a pot of boiling water. It became obvious that she could no longer take care of herself. She is now living in a group home for elderly people.

many of the oldest-old lose their ability to live independently, and many require some form of long-term care, which can include nursing homes, assisted living facilities, in-home care, and specialized hospitals.

The significant costs associated with providing this support may need to be borne by families and society. And as fewer and fewer adult children are able or want to stay home to care for older relatives, the shift to institutional care for elders will represent an immense social change, especially in those cultures where older generations have traditionally lived with younger ones. And the more residents of developing countries seek jobs in cities or other areas far from where they grew up, the less access to informal family care their older relatives back home will have.

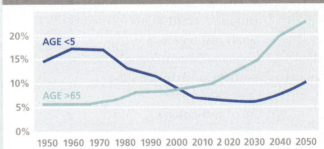

YOUNGER AND OLDER PEOPLE AS A PERCENT OF WORLDWIDE POPULATION BY DECADE

C **SUMMARIZE** In your own words, summarize the changes described in the article.

D **UNDERSTAND MEANING FROM CONTEXT** Paraphrase the statements, based on your understanding of the underlined words and phrases.

1 The world is facing a huge demographic shift.
2 These changes are without precedent.
3 We soon will have more elderly people than children.
4 And the older people get, the higher the prevalence of dementia.
5 Many of the oldest of the elderly population lose their ability to live independently.
6 Many require some form of long-term care.
7 Institutional care for the elderly will represent an immense social change.

E CRITICAL THINKING Choose the best answer about the future, based on information in the report.

1 Who will pay for long-term care of people who can no longer live independently?
   a Stay-at-home adults.
   b Families and society.
   c Older people themselves.

2 Why will fewer old people be able to get informal home care?
   a Because their younger relatives may have moved elsewhere.
   b Because there will be more institutional care available for them.
   c Because they will seek work.

F DRAW CONCLUSIONS Based on information in the report, what challenges do you think you will face as the people in your immediate or extended family age?

NOW YOU CAN Discuss caring for the elderly

A FRAME YOUR IDEAS With a partner, discuss these statements and check those you think are true about care for the elderly in your country.

- ☐ Most elderly people are adequately cared for.
- ☐ The way the elderly are cared for has been changing.
- ☐ The elderly usually live with younger family members.
- ☐ The elderly usually live in their own homes or apartments.
- ☐ The elderly usually live in special nursing homes.
- ☐ The government makes sure the elderly have affordable care.
- ☐ Younger people accept care for elderly relatives as their responsibility.
- ☐ Older people generally prefer not to socialize with younger people.
- ☐ Other: ....

B PAIR WORK With a partner, discuss the challenges each person is facing and recommend solutions.

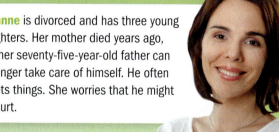

Suzanne is divorced and has three young daughters. Her mother died years ago, and her seventy-five-year-old father can no longer take care of himself. He often forgets things. She worries that he might get hurt.

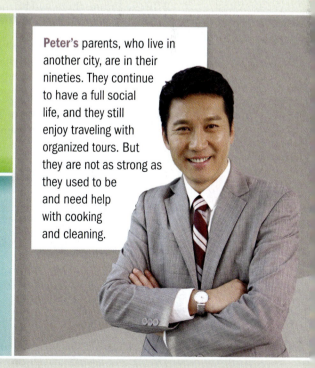

Peter's parents, who live in another city, are in their nineties. They continue to have a full social life, and they still enjoy traveling with organized tours. But they are not as strong as they used to be and need help with cooking and cleaning.

David and his wife have two children and live in a small two-bedroom apartment. They both work long hours to make ends meet. David's mother just turned eighty and lives alone. David is concerned about his mother's well-being.

C DISCUSSION How do you think the elderly will be cared for by the time you are old? How would *you* like to be cared for? Use Frame Your Ideas for support.

WRITING: Avoiding run-on sentences and comma splices

A **WRITING SKILL** Study the rules.

Note two common errors that writers often make when joining two sentences:

Run-on sentences (connecting sentences or independent clauses without using punctuation)
   INCORRECT: My grandmother was strict with my mom however, my mom isn't at all strict with me.

Comma splices (connecting two sentences or independent clauses with a comma and no conjunction)
   INCORRECT: My dad and I used to have lots of arguments, now we get along great.

To correct a run-on sentence or a comma splice, choose one of the following techniques:

- Use a period, and capitalize the following word.
  - My grandmother was strict with my mom. However, my mom isn't at all strict with me.
  - My dad and I used to have lots of arguments. Now we get along great.

- Use a semicolon.
  - My grandmother was strict with my mom; my mom isn't at all strict with me.
  - My dad and I used to have lots of arguments; now we get along great.

- Use a comma and a coordinating conjunction.
  - My grandmother was strict with my mom, but my mom isn't at all strict with me.
  - My dad and I used to have lots of arguments, but now we get along great.

Coordinating conjunctions			
and	for	or	yet
but	nor	so	

B **PRACTICE** All the sentences have errors. Label each sentence R (for run-on) or C (for comma splice). Then, on a separate sheet of paper, correct each sentence, using one of the techniques.

.... 1 Older people will use a lot of societal resources in the future, they will require caregivers and special institutions.

.... 2 In the future, there will be many more people in the oldest demographic however, we expect to have more treatments for some of their most common ailments.

.... 3 I worry a lot about my grandparents they both have had diabetes for many years.

.... 4 It's very difficult for my mother to stay home to care for my great-grandfather, he needs care because he has Alzheimer's disease.

C **PRACTICE** On a separate sheet of paper, rewrite the paragraph, correcting any run-on sentences or comma splices.

> My husband and I don't know what to do with our teenage daughter, Beth. Beth has always been a bit rebellious however, lately her behavior has really been going downhill. Yesterday, Beth's teacher told us that she was disrespectful in class she hadn't done her homework. We're at our wits' end with her. At home Beth has developed a spoiled attitude, she isn't willing to help at all. She used to make her bed and clean up her room, recently she has been leaving her things everywhere. My husband and I may have been too lenient with Beth as she was growing up, now that she's a teenager we have to get her to shape up.

D **APPLY THE WRITING SKILL**
Write a blog post with advice for parents and teens who don't have a good relationship. Use the vocabulary and expressions from this unit. Write at least three paragraphs, each one with a topic sentence stating its main idea.

SELF-CHECK
☐ Did I avoid run-on sentences and comma splices?
☐ Do all the sentences support the topic sentence?
☐ Did I use the vocabulary and expressions I learned in this unit?

REVIEW

A ▶ 4:24 Listen to the conversations about generational issues. Then listen to each conversation again and complete the statement with the correct comparative.

1 Jordan has been spending …… time on the Internet.
   a more and more
   b less and less

2 …… , the more her mother worries.
   a The later Sandi stays out
   b The older Sandi gets

3 The stricter Jill's father gets, …… she becomes.
   a the more rebellious
   b the more spoiled

4 The older the sisters get, …… .
   a the smarter they become
   b the more they appreciate their parents

B Write the adjective that best describes the behavior in each statement.

1 Mark's parents don't allow him to watch more than two hours of TV a day, but most of his friends can watch as much as they want. He feels that his parents are …………………… .

2 Karen has a closet full of expensive clothes, yet she always complains about not having anything to wear. Her parents usually buy her whatever she wants. A lot of people think Karen is …………………… .

3 Even though she has had her driver's license for a year and a half, Marissa's parents worry about her driving at night. They say that it's too dangerous, but Marissa thinks they're just being …………………… .

4 When Clyde's grandfather asked him to turn down the volume of his music, he ignored him. Clyde's grandfather thought this was very …………………… .

5 Rodney and Carolyn believe parents don't need to be so concerned about their children. They rarely set rules for their kids. Carolyn's sister thinks this is a bad idea. She feels they're …………………… .

6 Deanna wears clothing that her parents find shocking. She also has friends that her parents don't approve of. Her mother wishes she weren't so …………………… .

C Read the sentences. If the underlined word is in the incorrect part of speech, correct it.

1 Teenagers were given a lot more <u>responsibility</u> when I was young.
2 I think teenagers today lack the <u>mature</u> to make decisions for themselves.
3 The main reason young people are rebellious today is <u>selfishness</u>.
4 If kids today were taught about <u>courteous</u>, they would be better behaved.
5 There's no question that teenagers today demand more <u>independent</u> than they did fifty years ago.
6 It's important for parents to be involved in their children's <u>development</u>.
7 Young people have a lot more <u>mobile</u> than they did several generations ago.
8 It seems like there's a lot more <u>rebellious</u> among teenagers today.

TEST-TAKING SKILLS BOOSTER   p. 158

Web Project: Elder Care
www.english.com/summit3e

UNIT 9

Facts, Theories, and Hoaxes

COMMUNICATION GOALS
1. Speculate about everyday situations
2. Present a theory
3. Discuss how believable a story is
4. Evaluate the trustworthiness of news sources

PREVIEW

A FRAME YOUR IDEAS Take the quiz with a partner and discuss your answers.

THE WORLD'S EASIEST QUIZ... OR IS IT?

Be careful: The answers may seem obvious, but they might not be what you think! Will you "take a wild guess" by closing your eyes and just choosing A, B, C, or D? Or will you use "the process of elimination" by rejecting the answers that can't possibly be true?

1 How long did the Hundred Years' War in Western Europe last?
- A 100 years
- B 116 years
- C 50 years
- D 200 years

2 Where do Panama hats come from?
- A Panama
- B The Philippines
- C Ecuador
- D Italy

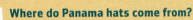

3 From which animals do we get catgut for violin strings?
- A cats
- B sheep
- C sharks
- D dogs

4 The former U.S.S.R. used to celebrate the October Revolution in which month?
- A October
- B November
- C December
- D June

5 What is a camel hair paintbrush made of?
- A camel hair
- B squirrel hair
- C cat hair
- D human hair

6 The Canary Islands in the Atlantic Ocean are named after which animal?
- A the canary
- B the cat
- C the dog
- D the camel

7 What was King George VI of England's first name?
- A George
- B Charles
- C Joseph
- D Albert

8 What color is a male purple finch?
- A dark purple
- B pinkish-red
- C sky blue
- D white

9 What country do Chinese gooseberries come from?
- A China
- B Japan
- C Sweden
- D New Zealand

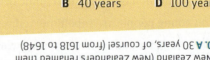

10 How long did the Thirty Years' War in Central Europe last?
- A 30 years
- B 40 years
- C 20 years
- D 100 years

SCORING

1–2 CORRECT We TOLD you they weren't so easy!

3–5 CORRECT Not bad! Did you already know a few of the answers?

6–10 CORRECT Either you're a great guesser, or you're a true scholar!

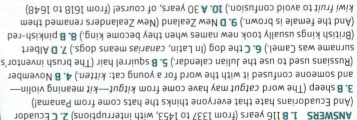

ANSWERS: 1. **B** 116 years (from 1337 to 1453, with interruptions) 2. **C** Ecuador (And Ecuadorians hate that everyone thinks the hats come from Panama!) 3. **B** sheep (The word *catgut* may have come from *kitgut*—*kit* meaning violin—and someone confused it with the word for a young cat: *kitten*.) 4. **B** November (Russians used to use the Julian calendar.) 5. **B** squirrel hair (The brush inventor's surname was Camel.) 6. **C** the dog (In Latin, *canarias* means dogs.) 7. **D** Albert (British kings usually took new names when they become king.) 8. **B** pinkish-red (And the female is brown.) 9. **D** New Zealand (New Zealanders renamed them *kiwi fruit* to avoid confusion.) 10. **A** 30 years, of course! (from 1618 to 1648)

B DISCUSSION Did you have a reason for each answer you chose? Did you just take wild guesses, or did you use the process of elimination? Which method do you think works better? Why?

C ▶ 5:01 **SPOTLIGHT** Read and listen to a conversation about a mystery. Notice the spotlighted language.

ENGLISH FOR TODAY'S WORLD
Understand a variety of accents.
Boris = Russian
Tina = Korean

Boris: Have you been keeping up with all the news about that missing military jet?
Tina: Yeah. Very mysterious, don't you think? The whole thing **doesn't make sense**.
Boris: No, it doesn't. I mean, how can a military plane just **vanish without a trace** over the Mediterranean Sea? Where's the evidence of a crash?
Tina: I have no idea, but apparently there was bad weather. Most likely the pilot lost control and it crashed into the water.
Boris: They claim that's the probable explanation but, in my opinion, they**'re barking up the wrong tree**.
Tina: What do you mean?
Boris: Well, I know **I'm going out on a limb** with this, but the plane might have been taken over by someone and flown to a secret location.
Tina: Oh come on! How could anyone take over a military plane? You **don't really buy that**, do you?
Boris: Why not? Rumor has it that there were two high-level government scientists aboard. Maybe someone wanted the information they might have had.
Tina: I'm sorry, but that seems really **far-fetched to me**. It's just not believable! There's no question the plane crashed. The only question is where.

D **UNDERSTAND IDIOMS AND EXPRESSIONS** With a partner, find these expressions in Spotlight and discuss the meaning of each. Explain what it means when…

1 something "doesn't make sense"
2 something "vanishes without a trace"
3 someone "barks up the wrong tree"
4 someone "goes out on a limb"
5 someone "doesn't buy" an idea
6 something seems "far-fetched"

E **DISCUSSION** Discuss the questions with a partner.
1 Do you think Boris's theory is far-fetched? Why or why not?
2 Do you generally believe what you hear or read in the news? Why or why not?

SPEAKING

A **PAIR WORK** Read each rumor and discuss how believable you think it is. Explain your reasons, using the expressions from Exercise D.

	most likely true	might be true	doesn't make sense	sounds far-fetched
1 That vaccines cause physical harm to young children	○	○	○	○
2 That the British monarchy controls the world's economy	○	○	○	○
3 That aliens from other planets have visited Earth	○	○	○	○
4 That the 1969 moon landing never actually happened	○	○	○	○

B **DISCUSSION** Which did you find more difficult to do: express an opinion on the rumors in Exercise A, or answer the questions in the quiz on page 98? Why?

LESSON 1

GOAL Speculate about everyday situations

A ▶5:02 **VOCABULARY** **DEGREES OF CERTAINTY** Read and listen. Then listen again and repeat.

I wonder what happened to Clare.

very certain	
Clearly, It's obvious (that) There's no question (that)	she got stuck in traffic.

almost certain	
Most likely Probably I'll bet I suppose	she got stuck in traffic.

not certain	
Maybe It's possible (that) I wonder if	she got stuck in traffic.

B ▶5:03 **LISTEN TO ACTIVATE VOCABULARY** Listen to each conversation and circle the phrase that best completes the statement. Then explain your choices.

1 She is (very certain / almost certain / not certain) about the reason Jade got grounded.
   He is (very certain / almost certain / not certain) about the reason Jade got grounded.
2 She is (very certain / almost certain / not certain) about the reason Jack is in debt.
   He is (very certain / almost certain / not certain) about the reason Jack is in debt.
3 She is (very certain / almost certain / not certain) why Linda got her kids a puppy.
   He is (very certain / almost certain / not certain) why Linda got her kids a puppy.

C **APPLY THE VOCABULARY** Write three sentences about each situation, each with a different degree of certainty. (a = very certain, b = almost certain, c = not certain) Compare sentences with a partner.

1 You're trying to take the elevator downstairs to get some lunch. You've been waiting for the elevator for over ten minutes.

a *Clearly, the elevator isn't working.*
b ....
c ....

2 It's 9:30, and your teacher hasn't arrived yet for your 9:00 class.

a ....
b ....
c ....

3 You go to your favorite restaurant. The lights are on, but the doors are locked, and there's no one inside.

a ....
b ....
c ....

4 You expected a package to arrive on Monday. It's Friday, and it still hasn't come.

a ....
b ....
c ....

NOW YOU CAN Speculate about everyday situations

A ▶ 5:04 **CONVERSATION SPOTLIGHT** Read and listen. Notice the spotlighted conversation strategies.

A: **I wonder** where Stacey is. She said she'd be here by ten.
B: Do you think something happened?
A: No idea. But **I'm sure it's nothing.** I'll bet she got stuck in traffic.
B: **I suppose you're right.** But I'm surprised she hasn't called.
A: I am, too.
B: **There must be a good explanation.** Maybe she left her phone at home.
A: Could be. I forget mine all the time.

▶ 5:06 **Ways to say "I don't know."**
No idea.
No clue.
Beats me.

▶ 5:07 **Responding to speculation**
Could be.
Maybe.
I suppose.

B ▶ 5:05 **RHYTHM AND INTONATION** Listen again and repeat. Then practice the conversation with a partner.

C **CONVERSATION ACTIVATOR** Create a similar conversation, using one of the situations in Exercise C on pages 100–101 (or another situation.) Start like this: *I wonder …* Be sure to change roles and then partners.

DON'T STOP!
- Continue to speculate, using varying degrees of certainty.
- Say as much as you can.

RECYCLE THIS LANGUAGE
- It doesn't make sense.
- I don't buy that.
- That sounds far-fetched.
- There's no question…

101

LESSON 2

GOAL Present a theory

A ▶ 5:08 **GRAMMAR SPOTLIGHT** Read about Rapa Nui. Notice the spotlighted grammar.

ISLAND OF MYSTERY

Rapa Nui (or Easter Island) is the most remote inhabited island in the world. Its huge stone figures (called *moai*) are world-famous, but their origin, as well as much of the island's history, is shrouded in mystery.

Experts believe the stone figures **may have been used** to establish religious and political authority and power, but no one knows for sure. Islanders moved a total of 540 figures across the island—some as far as 22 kilometers. Several experts believe the *moai* **could have been "walked"** upright, using ropes to rock the figures back and forth. Others theorize the islanders **must have laid** the figures down flat and **rolled** them over logs. They point out that moving each figure **could not have been accomplished** without the help of 70 or more people and probably took days to achieve.

In the early twentieth century, Norwegian explorer Thor Heyerdahl noticed cultural similarities between the people on Rapa Nui and the Incas in Peru. He argued that the island **might have been inhabited** by people who came in boats from South America. To prove it was possible, he successfully sailed a raft called the Kon-Tiki on that route. However, experts citing more recent DNA evidence confirmed that the original inhabitants **had to have sailed** from Polynesia, which lies to the west.

The first arrivals most likely found an inviting habitat lush with palm forests. However, today, the native trees are extinct. Some experts believe that, as the population of this small island increased, trees **must have been cut** down to build houses and boats and to make logs for moving the huge *moai*.

These are some of the theories about Rapa Nui, its stone figures, and the people who created them. Perhaps someday we will learn all the answers.

the Kon-Tiki

B **DRAW CONCLUSIONS** Which theory of how the *moai* were moved seems most believable to you? Explain your reasons.

C **GRAMMAR** PERFECT MODALS FOR SPECULATING ABOUT THE PAST: ACTIVE AND PASSIVE VOICE

Active voice
You can form perfect modals using <u>may</u>, <u>might</u>, <u>could</u>, <u>must</u>, or <u>had to</u> to speculate with different degrees of certainty about the past. Remember: A perfect modal is formed with a modal + <u>have</u> and a past participle.

very certain:	The islanders **had to have come** from Polynesia.
	They **couldn't** (or **can't**) **have come** from Peru.
almost certain:	The figures **must have been** very important.
	They **must not have been** easy to move.
not certain:	They **might** (or **may**) **have moved** the *moai* by "walking" them.
	However, they also **could have laid** the *moai* flat on logs.

Passive voice
Use the passive voice if the performer of the action is unknown or if you want to focus on the receiver of the action. To form the passive voice with perfect modals, use a modal + <u>have been</u> and a past participle. In negative statements, place <u>not</u> before the auxiliary <u>have</u>.

The stone figures **must have been moved** using ropes and logs.
The secrets of Rapa Nui **might not have been lost** if their writing system had survived.
The island **couldn't have been inhabited** originally by people from South America.

PRONUNCIATION BOOSTER p. 149
Reduction and linking in perfect modals in the passive voice

GRAMMAR BOOSTER p. 138
Perfect modals: short responses (active and passive voice)

D **UNDERSTAND THE GRAMMAR** Read the Grammar Spotlight again. Circle the perfect modals that are in the active voice. Underline those that are in the passive voice.

E **GRAMMAR PRACTICE** On a separate sheet of paper, rewrite the sentences with perfect modals in the active voice.

1. Scientists believe that <u>it's possible some form of life existed</u> on the planet Mars billions of years ago.

   > Scientists believe that some form of life could have existed on the planet Mars billions of years ago.

2. Heyerdahl thought <u>it was possible that they had come</u> on a raft like the Kon-Tiki.
3. Some historians think that <u>the Rapa Nui islanders probably didn't move</u> the *moai* using logs.
4. <u>It's possible someone forced the pilot</u> to fly the plane to a different location.
5. Experts suggest that originally <u>the Rapa Nui people most likely wrote</u> on banana leaves.
6. <u>There's no question that hunting was</u> the cause of the carrier pigeon's extinction as a species.

F **GRAMMAR PRACTICE** Complete the conversations, using perfect modals in the passive voice.

Harvard Professor Claims Egyptian Pyramids Built by Aliens from Space

1. **A:** I suppose they ………………………… by aliens.
   B: Come on! You don't really buy that, do you?

New Zealand Scientist Argues Dinosaurs Killed by Giant Tsunami

2. **A:** That sounds far-fetched to me. I think the dinosaurs ………………………… by something else.
   B: I suppose you're right.

SHOCKING NEW REVELATION: Artist Vincent van Gogh was actually murdered by brother

3. **A:** Do you think that's possible?
   B: Of course not. He ………………………… by his brother. Everyone knows he killed himself!

Woman Attacked by Lion While Shopping in London

4. **A:** That just doesn't make sense!
   B: Don't be so sure. Someone ………………………… by a lion if it had escaped from the zoo.

NOW YOU CAN Present a theory

A **FRAME YOUR IDEAS** Read about each mystery. On a separate sheet of paper, write a theory to explain each one, using perfect modals. Your theories can be believable or far-fetched.

The Yeti For centuries, people in Asia's remote Himalayan Mountains have claimed to have seen a shy, hairy, human-like creature. However, no one has ever captured a yeti or taken its photo. These sightings continue to be reported today.

Stonehenge Stonehenge was built over 3,000 years ago in England. Experts say the huge stones came from mountains 257 kilometers away. No one knows for sure how the stones were carried or put into place. The purpose of the stones is unknown.

The Nazca Lines These huge shapes were carved into the earth in Peru more than 1,500 years ago and can only be seen from an airplane. No one knows how they were designed or made.

 B **DISCUSSION ACTIVATOR** Speculate about each mystery, using active or passive perfect modals when possible. Use Degrees of Certainty vocabulary from page 100. Say as much as you can.

> 66 I believe the stones at Stonehenge **may have been used** for religious purposes. That's what makes the most sense to me. 99

C **PRESENTATION** Choose one of the mysteries. Present the theory that you think best explains the mystery and tell the class why you believe it.

LESSON 3

GOAL Discuss how believable a story is

A READING WARM-UP What kind of information would you need to determine whether or not a news story is true?

B ▶ 5:09 READING Read the article. Which details do you think are the most questionable or the least believable?

THE ROSWELL INCIDENT

On June 25th 1947, pilot Kenneth Arnold was flying a plane in the northwest of the U.S. when he saw something strange: objects that looked like plates, or saucers, flying across the sky like a small flock of birds. His story led to numerous other news stories in which people claimed to have seen similar unidentified flying objects (UFOs)—or "flying saucers."

A weather balloon

Shortly after, on July 8th, a secret military balloon crashed near Roswell, New Mexico, in the southwest. However, the local newspaper reported that a flying saucer had crashed, and the news media from all over demanded more information. Because the balloon was a secret, the military made an official announcement: that the object that had crashed was just an ordinary weather balloon.

No one questioned that story for more than thirty years—until 1978. UFO lecturer Stanton Friedman interviewed a man who claimed to have seen something stranger than a weather balloon in the wreckage of the 1947 crash, and the story of a flying saucer was reborn. Although versions of that story differ, most people who believe there was a military conspiracy to hide the truth agree on these basic details: a flying saucer crashed near Roswell in 1947. And because it didn't want anyone to know the truth, the military kept the incident top secret and continues to do so today.

However, many details have been added to the story over the years. Eleven additional "crash sites" have been identified. While some people claim that alien beings from other planets must have been captured alive and imprisoned by the military in a secret location, others believe that aliens might have died in the crash and were most likely being kept frozen for research. Roswell conspiracy fans meet at annual conferences to debate the various versions.

The military eventually admitted that it had been a secret military balloon. However, Roswell "experts" claim to have interviewed hundreds of witnesses who say they saw evidence of a flying saucer, proving, therefore, that the conspiracy theory must be true. B.D. Gildenberg, who has examined such claims, believes that the Roswell conspiracy stories are a hoax—"the world's most famous, most exhaustively investigated, and most thoroughly debunked UFO claim." Other skeptics of the conspiracy, who accept the military's version, point out that all the interviews occurred more than thirty years after the crash and that many of the statements made in the interviews were highly questionable. For example, one witness's name was changed after it became clear that she didn't exist. Furthermore, witnesses often seemed to confuse details with military plane crashes that had occurred in the area at about the same time.

Attendees at annual "Roswell" conferences debate conflicting theories about alien visitors and UFOs.

All the same, a CNN / *Time* poll in the U.S. showed that a majority of the people who responded found the UFO story very believable. Conspiracy critic Kal Korff admits, "Let's not pull any punches here: The Roswell UFO myth has been very good business for UFO groups, publishers, Hollywood, the town of Roswell, [and] the media."

C CONFIRM POINT OF VIEW Write A, B, or C to classify the people or organizations based on their point of view.

A = a skeptic of the military's version of the Roswell incident
B = a skeptic of the Roswell conspiracy theory
C = not enough information in the article to know for sure

1 .... Kenneth Arnold
2 .... Stanton Friedman
3 .... Roswell "experts"
4 .... Roswell conspiracy fans
5 .... CNN / *Time*
6 .... B.D. Gildenberg
7 .... Kal Korff

D **INFER INFORMATION** Based on information from the article, infer the answers to these questions.

1. What did Stanton Friedman's first witness probably tell him he saw in 1947?
2. When B.D. Gildenberg says the Roswell conspiracy is a "hoax," what does he mean?
3. When Kal Korff says the Roswell conspiracy is "very good business," what does he mean?
4. When the military finally admitted years later that they hadn't told the truth about the weather balloon in 1947, how would you guess Roswell conspiracy fans responded?

E ▶ 5:10 **WORD STUDY** **ADJECTIVES WITH THE SUFFIX -ABLE** Listen and repeat.

believable	can be accepted as true because it seems possible
debatable	more than one explanation is possible
unprovable	cannot be shown to be true
questionable	likely to be untrue

F **WORD STUDY PRACTICE** Use the adjectives from Exercise E to complete each statement.

1. His story is really .... So many of the details sound far-fetched.
2. I think she's telling the truth. Her description of the events sounds very .... to me.
3. Your claims are .... It isn't difficult to find another explanation for what happened.
4. That the military found a flying saucer is .... There is no evidence to show that they did.

NOW YOU CAN Discuss how believable a story is

A **NOTEPADDING** With a partner, create a story for each of two imaginary witnesses of the 1947 Roswell event: one supporting the conspiracy theory and one supporting the military's version.

Witness	What did the witness claim to have seen or heard?
1 a bus driver	He saw a flying saucer on the road. Some injured aliens were lying on the ground nearby. Some soldiers were …

Witness	What did the witness claim to have seen or heard?
1	
2	

B **GAME** **"TO TELL THE TRUTH"** Divide the class into two opposing groups. Group A will argue that there was a Roswell conspiracy. Group B will defend the military's version. Students from each group role-play the witnesses, making their stories as believable as possible. Students in the opposing group ask questions in order to determine if the witness is telling the truth.

❝ How many aliens did you see? ❞

❝ What did they look like? ❞

C **DISCUSSION** Vote to decide which witnesses told the most believable stories. Explain your reasons.

RECYCLE THIS LANGUAGE
- It doesn't make sense.
- I don't buy that.
- You're barking up the wrong tree.
- [You] really went out on a limb.
- That's just far-fetched.
- There's no question…

❝ I thought the first witness's story was **questionable** because he must have … ❞

LESSON 4

GOAL Evaluate the trustworthiness of news sources

A **LISTENING WARM-UP** **DISCUSSION** Look at the photo. Speculate about the purpose of the object behind the people.

Falcon Heene (front left) with his parents, Richard and Mayumi, and his brothers.

B ▶ 5:11 **LISTEN FOR MAIN IDEAS** Listen to Part 1 of this true story and discuss the questions.

1 What was the story that was being reported in the news?
2 Why did the Heene family contact the authorities?
3 What happened to the balloon?
4 What surprise did everyone discover afterward?

C ▶ 5:12 **LISTEN TO DRAW CONCLUSIONS** Listen to Part 2 of the story. Complete the statements. Explain your choices.

1 News agencies grew suspicious about the story because ....
   a Falcon's father answered interviewers' questions
   b Falcon got sick during the interviews

2 Authorities grew suspicious when they learned about Falcon's father's ....
   a interests
   b inventions

3 A publicity stunt is when someone tries to ....
   a hide the truth from the authorities
   b get the attention of the media

4 Falcon's parents agreed to pay $36,000 as ....
   a a donation
   b a punishment

D **CRITICAL THINKING** Discuss these questions. Listen to Part 2 again if necessary.

1 Do you think the authorities should have been less lenient or more lenient toward Falcon's parents? Why or why not?
2 Do you agree that the media probably made errors in judgment in the way they reported the story? Explain your opinion.
3 Do you think the media generally do a good job reporting the news? Provide examples of good or bad reporting.

NOW YOU CAN Evaluate the trustworthiness of news sources

A **FRAME YOUR IDEAS** Complete the survey and calculate your score. Then compare results with a partner. Which one of you is generally more skeptical?

ARE YOU A *skeptic?*

NOT SKEPTICAL ← → VERY SKEPTICAL

100% 90% 70% 50% 30% 10% 0%

- What percentage of the news you read in the newspaper do you think is true?
- What percentage of the news you hear on TV or radio do you think is true?
- What percentage of what you see on the Internet do you think is true?
- What percentage of what politicians say do you think is true?
- What percentage of what advertisers say do you think is true?
- What percentage of what your family says do you think is true?
- What percentage of what your friends say do you think is true?

HOW SKEPTICAL ARE YOU?
First add up all the percentage numbers you checked to get your total. Then calculate your average score by dividing your total by 7.

TOTAL [ ]   AVERAGE SCORE [ ]

B **NOTEPADDING** On the notepad, write news sources you trust and ones you don't. Include sources from newspapers, magazines, TV, radio, and the Internet. Explain your reasons.

The news sources I trust the most	Some news sources I don't trust
Why?	Why not?

C **DISCUSSION** Why do you trust some news sources and not others? Do you and your classmates agree on any? How can you determine if the information you read or hear is true or not?

RECYCLE THIS LANGUAGE

- I'm sorry to say …
- I hate to say it, but …
- To tell you the truth, …
- Unfortunately, …
- The sad fact is …

- There's no question …
- I don't buy [that story].
- … doesn't make sense to me.
- They're barking up the wrong tree.
- They went out on a limb.

- believable
- questionable
- reliable
- troubling
- careful / careless
- disappointed / disappointing

OPTIONAL WRITING Write about a news source you trust, or one you don't trust. Explain your reasons.

WRITING: Avoiding sentence fragments

A WRITING SKILL Study the rules.

A sentence fragment is a group of words that does not express a complete thought. Here are two common fragments.

A dependent clause
A dependent clause is a group of words that contains both a subject and a verb but begins with a subordinating conjunction, making it an incomplete thought.

> FRAGMENT: ~~Because the military hadn't told the truth.~~
> FRAGMENT: ~~After his mother admitted to lying.~~

A phrase
A phrase is a group of words that is not a complete sentence. Common phrases are prepositional phrases, verb phrases, embedded questions, infinitive phrases, relative clauses, etc.

> FRAGMENT: ~~The people who were at the airport.~~
> FRAGMENT: ~~At the end of the year.~~
> FRAGMENT: ~~Are very reliable.~~
> FRAGMENT: ~~Where the balloon landed.~~
> FRAGMENT: ~~To solve the mystery.~~

Remember:
An independent clause ...
- contains a subject and a verb.
- expresses a complete thought.

A complete sentence ...
- starts with a capital letter.
- ends with a period.
- expresses a complete thought.
- needs at least one independent clause.

Subordinating conjunctions that begin a dependent clause

after	since
as soon as	unless
because	until
before	when
even though	whenever
if	while

To correct a sentence fragment, do one of the following:
- Attach a dependent clause to an independent clause to complete the thought.
  People believed the conspiracy theories because the military hadn't told the truth.
  After his mother admitted to lying, **everyone knew the story was a hoax**.

- Complete the thought by adding missing information to a phrase so it's a complete sentence.
  The people who were at the airport **couldn't board their planes**.
  They were freed from prison at the end of the year.
  Most newspapers are very reliable.
  That's where the balloon landed.
  To solve the mystery, **they interviewed all the witnesses**.

B PRACTICE Underline the sentence fragments in this paragraph. Then, on a separate sheet of paper, rewrite the paragraph correctly.

> When John Tyler did not appear at his wedding. His bride and the wedding guests were worried. They called the police for help. The police used helicopters. To search for John's car. An hour later, John called his bride by phone. She was shocked. Because John told her that he had been carjacked. According to his story. The carjackers had locked him in the trunk of his car. Meanwhile, the police had found John's car. In the parking lot of a hotel. Furthermore, John was found in a hotel room. Speaking with his wife on the phone. Apparently, he had been having doubts about getting married and had made up the whole story about the carjacking. John had to repay the town the $3,000 spent trying to rescue him during his carjacking hoax. He and his bride were married two weeks later.

C APPLY THE WRITING SKILL

On a separate sheet of paper, write a short news article about one of these topics:

a A real or imaginary mysterious event, such as a UFO sighting, a disappearance, or the discovery of a previously unknown place

b A real or imaginary story in which the media succeeded at telling, or failed to tell, the truth

SELF-CHECK
☐ Do all my sentences express complete thoughts?
☐ Did I avoid sentence fragments?
☐ Did I avoid run-on sentences?

REVIEW

A ▶ 5:13 Listen to the conversations. Then listen to each conversation again and choose the statement that is closer in meaning to what each person said.

1 The woman says ....
   a it's possible Bill overslept
   b Bill couldn't possibly have overslept

2 The woman says ....
   a it's possible the wallet is Gina's
   b it's almost certain that the wallet is Gina's

3 The man thinks ....
   a the president may have been involved in the scandal
   b the president had clearly been involved in the scandal

4 The man thinks ....
   a the story could possibly be a hoax
   b the story couldn't possibly be true

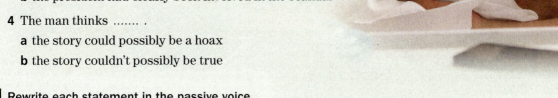

B Rewrite each statement in the passive voice.

1 The military must have moved the aliens' bodies to a secret place.
   ....

2 Witnesses might have seen evidence of the event.
   ....

3 Stanton Friedman must have written the first account of the Roswell conspiracy.
   ....

4 They couldn't have moved the stones without lots of help.
   ....

5 Richard Heene had to have asked Falcon to lie to the authorities.
   ....

6 The islanders might not have used the stone figures for religious purposes.
   ....

C On a separate sheet of paper, write your own response to each question, using varying degrees of certainty. Explain your theories.

1 Do you think it's possible that there could really be a human-like creature in the Himalayas called a yeti?

I suppose it's possible, but I really don't believe it because ...

2 Do you think the conspiracy theory about the Roswell incident could be true?
3 Does it make sense to you that the Bermuda Triangle might cause ships and planes to disappear?
4 Do you think it's possible that the Nazca Lines were designed by aliens?

TEST-TAKING SKILLS BOOSTER   p. 159

Web Project: Mysteries
www.english.com/summit3e

UNIT 10

Your Free Time

COMMUNICATION GOALS
1. Suggest ways to reduce stress
2. Describe how you got interested in a hobby
3. Discuss how mobile devices affect us
4. Compare attitudes about taking risks

PREVIEW

A **FRAME YOUR IDEAS** Complete the survey about your free time.

HOW DO YOU LIKE to spend your time?

RATE THESE ACTIVITIES ON A SCALE OF 0 TO 3.

- 3 = extremely important
- 2 = fairly important
- 1 = somewhat important
- 0 = not important to me at all

1. spending time with my family — 0 1 2 3
2. hanging out with my friends — 0 1 2 3
3. spending time alone relaxing and doing nothing — 0 1 2 3
4. immersing myself in my work or studies — 0 1 2 3
5. seeking excitement — 0 1 2 3
6. engaging in quiet activities at home — 0 1 2 3
7. participating in sports — 0 1 2 3
8. working out to stay in shape — 0 1 2 3
9. rooting for my favorite teams — 0 1 2 3
10. attending cultural events — 0 1 2 3
11. enjoying my hobbies and other interests — 0 1 2 3

B **PAIR WORK** Compare your survey responses. Ask questions about your partner's free time.

C   5:14 **VOCABULARY** **WAYS TO DESCRIBE PEOPLE** Listen and repeat. Then use the words and the survey to describe your partner.

- **sociable**: likes being around other people
- **a loner**: prefers being alone or hanging out with close friends or family
- **active**: enjoys doing lots of activities, has lots of interests
- **sedentary**: somewhat inactive physically
- **laid back**: relaxed, easygoing
- **other** ....

> "My partner is really sociable. She likes to spend time with her family and hang out with her friends."

D ▶5:15 **SPOTLIGHT** Read and listen to a conversation between two friends after work. Notice the spotlighted language.

ENGLISH FOR TODAY'S WORLD
Understand a variety of accents.
Ava = Arabic
Erin = American English (standard)

Ava: *[phone rings]* Don't you need to take that?
Erin: Nah. It's my new boss. It can wait till tomorrow.
Ava: Really? What if it's urgent?
Erin: She needs to know I'm not always **on call**. And besides, my workday ended over two hours ago … I have a life!
Ava: Well, you're a lot more laid back than I am. I've got **a lot on my plate** at work these days. I'd worry my boss might think I was **slacking off**.
Erin: But he knows that's not true! You work really hard.
Ava: I do. But I feel like I need to take my work home with me. Or I'll never be able to **keep up**.
Erin: Well, my previous boss was always calling me on the weekend. Finally, I had to put a stop to it. I just decided I wouldn't take any more calls after hours. You just have to **draw the line** somewhere, right?
Ava: I suppose so. But if I did that, I'd be **a nervous wreck** that I might lose my job.
Erin: Me, I can't live like that. When I'm at work, I **give it my all**. But my free time is mine … *[phone rings]* Is that yours?
Ava: I guess so … Oh no … I forgot I was supposed to call my boss at 7:00. Excuse me for a minute …
Erin: Come on! Don't tell me you're going to take that!
Ava: Stop that! Shhh!

E UNDERSTAND IDIOMS AND EXPRESSIONS Find these expressions in Spotlight. Match each with its correct meaning.

.... 1 be on call
.... 2 have a lot on one's plate
.... 3 slack off
.... 4 keep up
.... 5 draw the line
.... 6 be a nervous wreck
.... 7 give something one's all

a not work as hard as one should
b finish everything that needs to get done
c make it clear that something is unacceptable
d be anxious or worried about something
e make oneself available for someone to contact any time
f do something with maximum effort
g have lots of things that need to get done

F DISCUSSION Whose philosophy about taking work calls after hours makes the most sense to you — Ava's or Erin's? Explain your reasons.

SPEAKING **PAIR WORK** Complete the chart. Then tell your partner about the people. Use the Vocabulary from page 110.

❝ Unfortunately, Chris is a little sedentary because he's always immersed in his studies. ❞

Someone I know who …	Name	Relationship to you
is always immersed in his or her work or studies		
has a lot on his or her plate right now		
is good at drawing the line between work and private time		
maintains a very active life		
slacks off a little too often		
gives everything his or her all		

LESSON 1

GOAL Suggest ways to reduce stress

A ▶ 5:16 **VOCABULARY** **WAYS TO REDUCE STRESS** Read and listen to the suggestions for reducing the stress of work. Then listen again and repeat.

REDUCING THE STRESS OF WORK

 1 TAKE A BREATHER. Stop what you're doing from time to time. Take a rest or get some exercise.

 2 SET ASIDE SOME DOWN TIME. Schedule time that's just for you so you can focus on relaxing.

 3 SLOW DOWN. Don't do everything so fast. Take time to think about what you're doing and do it right.

 4 SET LIMITS. Learn to draw the line and say no to others' demands on your private time.

 5 LEARN TO LAUGH THINGS OFF. Stop taking things so seriously. Remember to see the humor in everything.

 6 TAKE UP A HOBBY. Start doing something you'd enjoy in your free time, such as making, collecting, fixing, or taking care of things.

B ▶ 5:17 **LISTEN TO ACTIVATE VOCABULARY** Read the suggestions. Then listen to six people's complaints. Write the number of a speaker in the box next to the suggestion you'd give him or her.

☐ "If I were you, I'd take a breather every few hours."
☐ "You should set aside some down time each week."
☐ "Slow down a bit so you can do the job right."
☐ "If I were you, I'd try to set some limits."
☐ "Why don't you try to laugh things off at work."
☐ "I think you should take up a hobby."

C **GRAMMAR** **EXPRESSING AN EXPECTATION WITH BE SUPPOSED TO**

Use **be supposed to** + a base form to express expectation. Use a present form of **be** for a present or future expectation. Use a past form of **be** for an expectation in the past.

We**'re supposed to arrive** on time today. (Someone expects it.)
Marcy **is supposed to bring** snacks tomorrow. (Someone will expect it.)
You **were supposed to come** yesterday. (Someone expected it.)

Negative statements
They **aren't supposed to know** about the party.
She **wasn't supposed to stay** past 5:00.

Yes / no questions
Is Paul **supposed to give** his presentation tomorrow?
Was the school **supposed to pay** you a refund?

Information questions
When **were** we **supposed to buy** the tickets?
Who**'s supposed to call** us today?

> **GRAMMAR BOOSTER** p. 139
> Be supposed to: expansion

> **Note:** The negative form of be supposed to can also express a prohibition.
> We're not supposed to text during class.

> **Be careful!**
> Don't use auxiliary verbs or modals with be supposed to.
>   Don't say: Marcy ~~will be~~ supposed to bring the snacks.
> Don't confuse be supposed to with the verb suppose.
>   I suppose I should call her. (= I assume I should.)
>   What do you suppose is wrong? (= What do you guess is wrong?)

D **UNDERSTAND THE GRAMMAR** Speculate about who might have an expectation.

1 Jeff is supposed to call home before he leaves the office.   *"His wife might expect it."*
2 Our teacher is supposed to tell us our final grades today.
3 Customers are supposed to leave a 15% tip after their meal.

E **ERROR CORRECTION** On a separate sheet of paper, rewrite these sentences correctly.
1 You don't suppose to smoke cigarettes inside the office.
2 Wasn't everyone suppose to turn off their phones during the talk?
3 Lena and Gil didn't supposed to finish their report before the meeting yesterday.
4 When will he be supposed to let his boss know he's taking time off?
5 What we suppose to do for tomorrow's class?

F **GRAMMAR PRACTICE** Rewrite each instruction to express an expectation, using **be supposed to**. Make any other necessary changes.

> **PRONUNCIATION BOOSTER** p. 150
> Vowel sounds /eɪ/, /ɛ/, /æ/, and /ʌ/

1 "Please bring your homework with you tomorrow."
(we / bring) ....
2 "Please tell Sara to call her mother after class."
(Sara / call) ....
3 "Please inform Walter that he needs to pay his bill by Friday."
(Walter / pay) ....
4 "Don't tell anyone about Tom's surprise birthday party on Sunday."
(I / tell) ....
5 "Don't tip people for their service when you're traveling in Japan."
(you / tip) ....
6 "All of our store clerks should be friendly, helpful, and courteous."
(Our store clerks / be) ....

NOW YOU CAN Suggest ways to reduce stress

A ▶5:18 **CONVERSATION SPOTLIGHT** Read and listen. Notice the spotlighted conversation strategies.

A: **Uh-oh**. I really messed up.
B: Why? What did you do?
A: **I just realized** we were supposed to turn in our reports this morning. It completely slipped my mind.
B: **Well, frankly,** I'm not surprised.
A: What do you mean?
B: **It's just that** you've been working so hard lately. **Let's face it** … you need a break.
A: You're probably right. I've got way too much on my plate.
B: **You know what?** It's time to slow down a little.

B ▶5:19 **RHYTHM AND INTONATION** Listen again and repeat. Then practice the conversation with a partner.

C **CONVERSATION ACTIVATOR** Create a similar conversation in which one of you is stressed out about forgetting to do something. Start like this: *Uh-oh. I really messed up…* Be sure to change roles and then partners.

Some ideas
You were supposed to …
• get someone a birthday gift.
• pick someone up at the airport.
• finish your homework.
• be at a meeting at work or school.
• prepare a presentation for an event.

DON'T STOP!
• Suggest and discuss other ways to reduce stress.
• Say as much as you can.

RECYCLE THIS LANGUAGE
• be on call
• be a nervous wreck
• can't keep up
• give it one's all
• draw the line

LESSON 2

GOAL Describe how you got interested in a hobby

A ▶5:20 **GRAMMAR SPOTLIGHT** Read about how these people got interested in their hobbies. Notice the spotlighted grammar.

ASSEMBLING MODELS

When I was a kid, I was crazy about airplanes. My dad did a lot of traveling for his job, so he **would bring** me back model kits from different airlines. I**'d assemble** them and paint them, and it was fun. My dad **was always showing** off my work to his friends, so I decided to get serious and make it a real hobby. Now I build my own models with engines that can really fly.

QUILTING

When I was young, my mom **was always collecting** old pieces of colorful cloth. At some point, she **would sew** them together into shapes, and then she **would combine** the shapes together to make a huge bed cover. I used to think it was embarrassing to have my friends come over and see all those pieces of cloth lying around. But today I'm really proud of the quilts my mom made.

PRACTICING A MARTIAL ART

When I was about eight, my friends were all learning martial arts. They**'d walk** past my house in their uniforms on their way to karate class, and I really wanted to join them. So I told my mom, and she agreed to let me. I've been practicing now for more than ten years. It's helped me to feel really confident physically.

B **PAIR WORK** With a partner, discuss which hobby in Exercise A is the most appealing to you. Explain your reasons.

GRAMMAR BOOSTER p. 139
- Would: review
- Placement of adverbs of manner

C **GRAMMAR** **DESCRIBING PAST REPEATED OR HABITUAL ACTIONS**

You can use would + a base form to describe past repeated or habitual actions.
  When I was a kid, my mom **would sew** pieces of cloth together to make quilts.
  Every weekend, I **would walk** around the neighborhood and take photos.

You can also use the past continuous with the frequency adverb always to describe a past habitual action.
  Our grandfather **was always fixing** things in his garage.
  We **were always taking care of** other people's pets.

Remember: You can also use used to + a base form to describe past habitual actions that are no longer true.
  My mom **used to make** quilts. [But she doesn't anymore.]
  I **used to love** assembling model cars. [But I don't have the time now.]

Be careful!
With non-action verbs that don't describe repeated actions, use used to, not would.
  We **used to be** interested in martial arts.
    NOT We ~~would be~~ interested in martial arts.
  She **used to dislike** sewing.
    NOT She ~~would dislike~~ sewing.

D NOTICE THE GRAMMAR Find an example of the past continuous with <u>always</u> in Spotlight on page 111. Restate the sentence, using <u>used to</u>.

E GRAMMAR PRACTICE Write an X next to the statements that cannot be rewritten using <u>would</u> for past repeated or habitual actions. Explain your decision for each item.

☐ 1 Nick used to like everything about going to school.
☐ 2 My brother used to collect soda cans when we were kids.
☐ 3 We used to visit antique stores to look for beautiful old things.
☐ 4 The prices of the model cars I liked the best used to be astronomical.
☐ 5 My family used to live next door to a karate school.
☐ 6 When Jan first started her new job, she used to immerse herself in her work.
☐ 7 When I was a teenager, I used to seek excitement by taking risks.

> *In item 1, <u>like</u> is a non-action verb. You can't use <u>would</u> for repeated actions with non-action verbs.*

F GRAMMAR PRACTICE On a separate sheet of paper, rewrite each statement from Exercise E that can be rewritten with <u>would</u>.

> *My brother would collect soda cans when we were kids.*

G GRAMMAR PRACTICE With a partner, take turns restating each statement from Exercise F, using the past continuous with <u>always</u>.

> *My brother was always collecting soda cans when we were kids.*

NOW YOU CAN Describe how you got interested in a hobby

A NOTEPADDING Using the Grammar Spotlight as a guide, write statements about one of your hobbies. Use <u>would</u> or the past continuous for past repeated or habitual actions when possible.

What is your hobby?
How did you first get interested in it?

How did your interest change over time?

B DISCUSSION ACTIVATOR Using your notepad, discuss your hobby with a partner. Find out about your partner's hobby. Say as much as you can.

C PRESENTATION With your partner, tell your class about how you each got interested in your hobbies.

OPTIONAL WRITING Write about how your partner got interested in his or her hobby.

LESSON 3

GOAL Discuss how mobile devices affect us

A **READING WARM-UP** Do you think technology increases or reduces stress in your life? Provide examples.

B ▶ 5:21 **READING** Read the article. How would you summarize the author's main points about technology today?

ALWAYS CONNECTED?
The Consequences of Never Switching Off
Alison Murphy

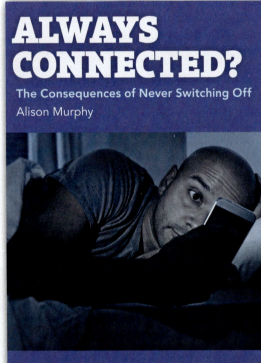

Advances in technology come with the promise of increased efficiency, making us more productive and providing more time to relax and enjoy our leisure time. However, some experts claim that the opposite is true—that we're actually working more and have less time to relax. And, as a result, we are becoming more stressed out.

Next time you're in a public place, look around. Odds are you'll see a large percentage of people on their phones or tablets texting, chatting, checking messages, or surfing the net. We're more connected to our mobile devices than ever before, which provides us 24/7 contact with our work, social media, and the Internet. The devices even follow us into our bedrooms, where we use technology as a means to unwind at the end of a long day.

According to a recent poll, a majority of respondents said they use their devices right before going to bed. Most also reported that using their devices keeps them up at night and that they don't get enough sleep. Zack Panatera, a student at Stanford University, complained, "I'll take a quick look at something interesting, and the next thing I know, I've spent a few hours online." According to psychiatrist Kyla Greenham, "The light from our devices throws off our normal sleep cycle and actually reduces production of the sleep hormone melatonin." She advises, "Switch off any kind of technology at least an hour before going to bed." Lack of sleep may not seem so important, but it can have a huge effect on one's performance the next day, making it harder to pay attention or remember things.

At work, technology is in fact a contributing factor in a growing trend toward longer hours and less time off. When we leave the office, we continue to stay connected. We are inviting our work world into our private lives in ways that never would have been imaginable in the past. We're constantly "on call," and our time is never entirely our own. We just don't know how to "switch off" our work when we get home.

In our leisure time, technology appears to be reducing the face-to-face human interaction that we've traditionally enjoyed. For example, the trend has been away from the shared experiences of going out to the movies or shopping at the mall, toward the more private acts of watching movies at home or shopping online. Common leisure activities of the past, such as participating in clubs, took place in the community and provided extended time to communicate with others and develop relationships. In contrast, today's online posts and tweets with family, friends, and colleagues are shorter, more superficial, and less satisfying. Recent research has in fact suggested that face-to-face family time is decreasing in homes with Internet connections.

No one wishes to turn back the clock on what technology can do. However, switching off our devices from time to time may be one of the most important decisions we can make to ensure that we are living full, satisfying lives.

C **UNDERSTAND MEANING FROM CONTEXT** With a partner, find these words and phrases in the article. Match each one with its correct meaning.

.... 1 switch off
.... 2 24/7
.... 3 a means to unwind
.... 4 keeps [someone] up at night
.... 5 lack of
.... 6 throws off
.... 7 face-to-face

a a way to relax
b all day and night
c insufficient amount or quantity
d prevents from sleeping
e by talking to someone directly, in person
f turn off
g makes something not work right

D IDENTIFY SUPPORTING DETAILS Answer the questions, according to the article. Find examples or information in the article to support your answers.
1. What is wrong with always being "on call" for an employer?
2. What are the consequences of checking one's devices before going to sleep?
3. Why is it a problem to rely on technology for social interaction?

E INFER POINT OF VIEW Answer the following questions. Explain your reasons.
1. What kinds of leisure activities do you think the author would recommend?
2. Do you think the author's opinion of electronic devices is more positive or negative? Explain.

DIGITAL EXTRA CHALLENGE

NOW YOU CAN Discuss how mobile devices affect us

4 = Frequently
3 = Somewhat frequently
2 = Once in a while
1 = Rarely
0 = Never

A FRAME YOUR IDEAS Complete the survey. Then compare answers with a partner. Describe your habits and explain why you do what you do.

HOW CONNECTED ARE YOU?

	0	1	2	3	4	not sure
I text to connect with other people.	○	○	○	○	○	○
I make calls to other people.	○	○	○	○	○	○
I stop whatever I'm doing to respond to calls or texts.	○	○	○	○	○	○
I check my messages as soon as I wake up.	○	○	○	○	○	○
I check my messages as soon as I get home.	○	○	○	○	○	○
I check my messages before going to sleep.	○	○	○	○	○	○
I wake up during the night and check my messages.	○	○	○	○	○	○
I switch off my devices during the day.	○	○	○	○	○	○
I switch off my devices at night.	○	○	○	○	○	○

BASED ON YOUR SURVEY RESPONSES, WHICH STATEMENT BELOW BEST DESCRIBES YOU?
- I'm almost always connected, and I think that's great.
- I'm almost always connected, but I wish I weren't.
- I think it's important to be connected, but I know when to switch off my devices.
- I'm hardly ever connected, but I wish I were more often.
- I'm hardly ever connected, and I'm glad.

B DISCUSSION Discuss the following questions in small groups. Then share your ideas with the class.
1. In your opinion, do technological advances save us time or waste more of our time? How?
2. What are your recommendations for the best ways to use our devices at work or school? In public places? At home?
3. Do you think technology adds to or interferes with your leisure time? Explain how.

" Texting keeps me in touch with more of my friends and makes it easier to get together. I don't think it interferes with my leisure time at all. "

LESSON 4

GOAL Compare attitudes about taking risks

A **LISTENING WARM-UP** **DISCUSSION** Which of the following risks would you find the easiest to take? Which would you find the most difficult? Explain your reasons.

Jumping out of an airplane

Changing your career after the age of 40

Driving way over the speed limit

Climbing a live volcano

B ▶ 5:22 **LISTEN FOR MAIN IDEAS** Listen to the interview with a psychologist. Then listen again and write a description for each of the two personality types the psychologist describes.

What is a "big T" personality?	What is a "small t" personality?

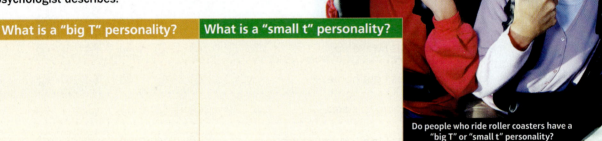
Do people who ride roller coasters have a "big T" or "small t" personality?

C ▶ 5:23 **LISTEN FOR SUPPORTING DETAILS** Read each summary of some of Franklin's main points. Listen again, and complete each explanation by providing details from the interview.

		Explanation
1	Franklin notes that one cannot simply classify people's personalities as either 100% "big T" or "small t."	
2	She clarifies that having a "big T" personality isn't always a positive trait.	
3	She argues that even if you are willing to ride on a roller coaster, you don't necessarily have a "big T" personality.	

D ▶ 5:24 **LISTEN TO UNDERSTAND MEANING FROM CONTEXT** Listen to each of the following comments from the interview and complete the statements.

1. If you are "faint of heart" and "wouldn't dare" to do certain things, you have more of a (big T / small t) personality.
2. A person who "takes chances" and chooses to "live on the edge" has more of a (big T / small t) personality.
3. If you feel an "adrenaline rush" when you go "right up to the edge," you have more of a (big T / small t) personality.

E **RELATE TO PERSONAL EXPERIENCE** Where do you fit on the risk-taking continuum? Do you have more of a "big T" or "small t" personality? Explain your reasons.

Risk-Avoider ⟶ Risk-Taker

F ▶ 5:25 **WORD STUDY   ADVERBS OF MANNER**
Most adverbs of manner are formed by adding -ly to an adjective. Listen and repeat.

Adjective		Adverb
confident	→	confident**ly**
mysterious	→	mysterious**ly**
quick	→	quick**ly**
quiet	→	quiet**ly**
safe	→	safe**ly**

Exceptions: If an adjective ends in ...
- -y, change to -ily. (nois**y** → nos**ily**)
- -l, add -ly. (carefu**l** → carefu**lly**)
- -ble, change to -bly. (comforta**ble** → comforta**bly**)

Usage note
Use an adverb of manner to modify a verb or adjective.
  Risk-taking affects you **physically**.
    [modifies the verb: describes how it affects you]
  I'm afraid of activities that are **physically** dangerous.
    [modifies the adjective: describes how they are dangerous]
Some adverbs such as luckily, fortunately, unfortunately, and sadly express the speaker's attitude. They are generally used at the beginning or end of a sentence.
  Luckily, no one was hurt. I was really frightened, **unfortunately**.

G **WORD STUDY PRACTICE**   Complete each statement, using an adverb of manner.

1 (dangerous) Many people who seek excitement like to live ....
2 (fortunate) My niece climbed a live volcano. Nothing terrible happened, ...
3 (easy) I don't like taking risks when I drive. Someone could .... get hurt.
4 (nervous) He .... checked his parachute before he jumped out of the plane.
5 (sad) .... , he was badly injured when he jumped off the cliff.
6 (extreme) The hike through the desert is .... challenging.
7 (beautiful) The stories about her adventures are .... written.
8 (accidental) She .... walked into a high-crime neighborhood.
9 (mysterious) Our teacher was .... absent over the last week.

NOW YOU CAN   Compare attitudes about taking risks

A **NOTEPADDING**   Interview a partner about the riskiest thing he or she has ever done. Take notes on your notepad. Use adverbs of manner if you can.

 B **DISCUSSION**   In small groups, compare your partners' experiences. Then decide who is the biggest risk-taker.

OPTIONAL WRITING   Write a paragraph about why you think a person becomes a risk-taker or a risk-avoider.

Name	Description of what happened:
Time and place	
Where?	

WRITING: Presenting and supporting opinions clearly

A WRITING SKILL Study the rules.

When you write to critique or comment on another person's ideas, it is important to present and support your own opinions clearly. Use connecting words and phrases to present your ideas logically, and support your ideas with reasons.

Present your ideas logically

First of all, I agree with Alison Murphy's main point.
In addition, she makes a good point about modern technology.
Furthermore, she's right about its effect on sleep.
Finally, I believe we need to decide what we want technology to do for us.

Support your ideas with reasons

Since they are able to work from home, people have more free time.
Because of the Internet, people are working more efficiently.
Actually, new technology increases leisure time. **That is why** I think the author is wrong.
Due to new technological advances, people are more connected than ever.

> **Citing the writer's words**
> Use direct speech to quote short statements.
> For example:
> *Murphy says, "It may be one of the most important decisions we can make."*
>
> For longer statements, use indirect speech to paraphrase what Murphy says.
> For example:
> *Murphy argues that technology is interfering with our sleep.*

B PRACTICE Write statements using the connecting words.

1 Smart phones are so convenient. It seems like everyone needs to have one. (since)
....

2 Online shopping is the reason fewer people shop at the mall these days. (because of)
....

3 Murphy's arguments are very strong. I agree with her opinions. (that is why)
....

4 The light from their devices is the reason people aren't getting enough sleep. (due to)
....

C PRACTICE On a separate sheet of paper, rewrite this paragraph by adding connecting words and phrases. Use a comma where necessary.

> **1** ……. I completely agree with Murphy when she suggests we switch off our devices more often. It's just common sense. **2** ……. I agree with her argument that our devices are keeping us up at night. **3** ……. I always check my messages before going to bed, I know exactly what she means. **4** ……. she makes a good point when she says that people are interacting face-to-face less and less. My family is trying to change that by setting aside family time. **5** ……. I think she's right when she says, "Switching off our devices may be one of the most important decisions we can make." **6** ……. I've decided to switch off my phone every evening at 7:00 P.M.

D APPLY THE WRITING SKILL Write a critique of the article "Always Connected?" on page 116. Begin by stating your opinion. To comment on the article's point of view, and to support yours, use quotes or paraphrase what the writer says. Write at least two paragraphs.
Idea: first, underline sentences in the article you want to comment on.

SELF-CHECK

☐ Did I use connecting words and phrases to present and support my opinions?
☐ Did I use quotation marks when citing the writer's own words?
☐ Did I paraphrase the writer's words when I didn't use direct speech?

REVIEW

A ▶ 5:26 Listen to the conversations. Complete each statement with the correct idiom or expression.

1 He has decided to ....
   a slack off   b draw the line   c be on call

2 She's ....
   a slacking off   b got a lot on her plate   c giving it her all

3 He's managing to ....
   a keep up   b be on call   c slack off

4 Her boss might think she was ....
   a keeping up   b giving it her all   c slacking off

B Use the prompts to write questions using <u>be supposed to</u>.

1 (we / read / the article before class tomorrow)
....

2 (why / I / contact / the authorities tomorrow morning)
....

3 (what / they / bring / to the party later tonight)
....

4 (what time / we / call / the office next Friday)
....

5 (how long / Daniel / stay at the library this afternoon)
....

6 (where / Lisa / go / tomorrow)
....

C Respond to each statement in your own words, using expressions from Preview or Lesson 1.

1 " Uh-oh. I really messed up. "   2 " I'm so sorry I forgot to call you! It completely slipped my mind. "   3 " Let's face it. You're working too hard. "

You: ....   You: ....   You: ....

D Write an adverb form for each adjective.

1 angry   ....   6 preferable   ....
2 busy   ....   7 respectful   ....
3 responsible   ....   8 honest   ....
4 appropriate   ....   9 polite   ....
5 happy   ....

TEST-TAKING SKILLS BOOSTER p. 160

Web Project: Extreme Sports
www.english.com/summit3e

Reference Charts

PRONUNCIATION TABLE

These are the pronunciation symbols used in *Summit 1*.

Vowels

Symbol	Key Word	Symbol	Key Word
i	beat, feed	ə	banana, among
ɪ	bit, did	ɚ	shirt, murder
eɪ	date, paid	aɪ	bite, cry, buy, eye
ɛ	bet, bed	aʊ	about, how
æ	bat, bad	ɔɪ	voice, boy
ɑ	box, odd, father	ɪr	beer
ɔ	bought, dog	ɛr	bare
oʊ	boat, road	ɑr	bar
ʊ	book, good	ɔr	door
u	boot, food, student	ʊr	tour
ʌ	but, mud, mother		

Consonants

Symbol	Key Word	Symbol	Key Word
p	pack, happy	z	zip, please, goes
b	back, rubber	ʃ	ship, machine, station, special, discussion
t	tie		
d	die		
k	came, key, quick	ʒ	measure, vision
g	game, guest	h	hot, who
tʃ	church, nature, watch	m	men, some
		n	sun, know, pneumonia
dʒ	judge, general, major		
		ŋ	sung, ringing
f	fan, photograph	w	wet, white
v	van	l	light, long
θ	thing, breath	r	right, wrong
ð	then, breathe	y	yes, use, music
s	sip, city, psychology	t̬	butter, bottle
		tˀ	button

IRREGULAR VERBS

base form	simple past	past participle	base form	simple past	past participle
be	was / were	been	forget	forgot	forgotten
beat	beat	beaten	forgive	forgave	forgiven
become	became	become	freeze	froze	frozen
begin	began	begun	get	got	gotten
bend	bent	bent	give	gave	given
bet	bet	bet	go	went	gone
bite	bit	bitten	grow	grew	grown
bleed	bled	bled	hang	hung	hung
blow	blew	blown	have	had	had
break	broke	broken	hear	heard	heard
breed	bred	bred	hide	hid	hidden
bring	brought	brought	hit	hit	hit
build	built	built	hold	held	held
burn	burned / burnt	burned / burnt	hurt	hurt	hurt
burst	burst	burst	keep	kept	kept
buy	bought	bought	know	knew	known
catch	caught	caught	lay	laid	laid
choose	chose	chosen	lead	led	led
come	came	come	leap	leaped / leapt	leaped / leapt
cost	cost	cost	learn	learned / learnt	learned / learnt
creep	crept	crept	leave	left	left
cut	cut	cut	lend	lent	lent
deal	dealt	dealt	let	let	let
dig	dug	dug	lie	lay	lain
do	did	done	light	lit	lit
draw	drew	drawn	lose	lost	lost
dream	dreamed / dreamt	dreamed / dreamt	make	made	made
drink	drank	drunk	mean	meant	meant
drive	drove	driven	meet	met	met
eat	ate	eaten	mistake	mistook	mistaken
fall	fell	fallen	pay	paid	paid
feed	fed	fed	put	put	put
feel	felt	felt	quit	quit	quit
fight	fought	fought	read /rid/	read /rɛd/	read /rɛd/
find	found	found	ride	rode	ridden
fit	fit	fit	ring	rang	rung
fly	flew	flown	rise	rose	risen
forbid	forbade	forbidden	run	ran	run

base form	simple past	past participle	base form	simple past	past participle
say	said	said	spring	sprang / sprung	sprung
see	saw	seen	stand	stood	stood
sell	sold	sold	steal	stole	stolen
send	sent	sent	stick	stuck	stuck
set	set	set	sting	stung	stung
shake	shook	shaken	stink	stank / stunk	stunk
shed	shed	shed	strike	struck	struck / stricken
shine	shone	shone	string	strung	strung
shoot	shot	shot	swear	swore	sworn
show	showed	shown	sweep	swept	swept
shrink	shrank	shrunk	swim	swam	swum
shut	shut	shut	swing	swung	swung
sing	sang	sung	take	took	taken
sink	sank	sunk	teach	taught	taught
sit	sat	sat	tear	tore	torn
sleep	slept	slept	tell	told	told
slide	slid	slid	think	thought	thought
smell	smelled / smelt	smelled / smelt	throw	threw	thrown
speak	spoke	spoken	understand	understood	understood
speed	sped / speeded	sped / speeded	upset	upset	upset
spell	spelled / spelt	spelled / spelt	wake	woke / waked	woken / waked
spend	spent	spent	wear	wore	worn
spill	spilled / spilt	spilled / spilt	weave	wove	woven
spin	spun	spun	weep	wept	wept
spit	spit / spat	spit / spat	win	won	won
spoil	spoiled / spoilt	spoiled / spoilt	wind	wound	wound
spread	spread	spread	write	wrote	written

STATIVE VERBS

amaze	desire	hear	need	seem	
appear*	dislike	imagine	owe	smell*	
appreciate	doubt	include*	own	sound	
astonish	envy	know	please	suppose	
be*	equal	like	possess	surprise	
believe	exist	look like	prefer	taste*	
belong	fear	look*	realize	think*	
care	feel*	love	recognize	understand	
consist of	forget	matter	remember*	want*	
contain	hate	mean	resemble	weigh*	
cost	have*	mind	see*		

*These verbs also have action meanings. Example: *I see a tree.* (non-action) *I'm seeing her tomorrow.* (action)

VERBS FOLLOWED BY A GERUND

acknowledge	consider	endure	imagine	prevent	resent
admit	delay	enjoy	justify	prohibit	resist
advise	deny	escape	keep	propose	risk
appreciate	detest	explain	mention	quit	suggest
avoid	discontinue	feel like	mind	recall	support
can't help	discuss	finish	miss	recommend	tolerate
celebrate	dislike	forgive	postpone	report	understand
complete	don't mind	give up	practice		

EXPRESSIONS THAT CAN BE FOLLOWED BY A GERUND

be excited about	be opposed to	believe in	blame [someone or something] for
be worried about	be used to	participate in	forgive [someone or something] for
be responsible for	complain about	succeed in	thank [someone or something] for
be interested in	dream about / of	take advantage of	keep [someone or something] from
be accused of	talk about / of	take care of	prevent [someone or something] from
be capable of	think about / of	insist on	stop [someone or something] from
be tired of	apologize for	look forward to	
be accustomed to	make an excuse for		
be committed to	have a reason for		

VERBS FOLLOWED DIRECTLY BY AN INFINITIVE

afford	choose	grow	mean	pretend	threaten
agree	claim	hesitate	need	promise	volunteer
appear	consent	hope	neglect	refuse	wait
arrange	decide	hurry	offer	request	want
ask	demand	intend	pay	seem	wish
attempt	deserve	learn	plan	struggle	would like
can't wait	expect	manage	prepare	swear	yearn
care	fail				

VERBS FOLLOWED BY AN OBJECT BEFORE AN INFINITIVE*

advise	choose*	force	need*	remind	urge
allow	convince	get*	order	request	want*
ask*	enable	help*	pay	require	warn
beg	encourage	hire	permit	teach	wish*
cause	expect*	instruct	persuade	tell	would like*
challenge	forbid	invite	promise*		

*In the active voice, these verbs can be followed by the infinitive without an object (example: *want to speak* or *want someone to speak*).

ADJECTIVES FOLLOWED BY AN INFINITIVE*

afraid	content	disturbed	glad	proud	sorry
alarmed	curious	eager	happy	ready	surprised
amazed	delighted	easy	hesitant	relieved	touched
angry	depressed	embarrassed	likely	reluctant	upset
anxious	determined	encouraged	lucky	sad	willing
ashamed	disappointed	excited	pleased	shocked	
certain	distressed	fortunate	prepared		

*Example: *I'm willing **to accept** that.*

VERBS THAT CAN BE FOLLOWED BY A GERUND OR AN INFINITIVE

with a change in meaning

forget (+ gerund)	=	forget something that happened
(+ infinitive)	=	forget something that needs to be done
regret (+ gerund)	=	regret a past action
(+ infinitive)	=	regret having to inform someone about an action
remember (+ gerund)	=	remember something that happened
(+ infinitive)	=	remember something that needs to be done
stop (+ gerund)	=	stop a continuous action
(+ infinitive)	=	stop in order to do something

without a change in meaning

begin	love
can't stand	prefer
continue	start
hate	try
like	

PARTICIPIAL ADJECTIVES

alarming	–	alarmed	disturbing	–	disturbed	paralyzing	– paralyzed
amazing	–	amazed	embarrassing	–	embarrassed	pleasing	– pleased
amusing	–	amused	entertaining	–	entertained	relaxing	– relaxed
annoying	–	annoyed	exciting	–	excited	satisfying	– satisfied
astonishing	–	astonished	exhausting	–	exhausted	shocking	– shocked
boring	–	bored	fascinating	–	fascinated	soothing	– soothed
comforting	–	comforted	frightening	–	frightened	startling	– startled
confusing	–	confused	horrifying	–	horrified	stimulating	– stimulated
depressing	–	depressed	inspiring	–	inspired	surprising	– surprised
disappointing	–	disappointed	interesting	–	interested	terrifying	– terrified
disgusting	–	disgusted	irritating	–	irritated	tiring	– tired
distressing	–	distressed	moving	–	moved	touching	– touched

SUMMIT 1B

Grammar Booster

Grammar Booster

The Grammar Booster is optional. It offers more information and extra practice, as well as Grammar for Writing. Sometimes it further explains or expands the unit grammar and points out common errors. In other cases, it reviews and practices previously learned grammar that would be helpful when learning new grammar concepts. If you use the Grammar Booster, you will find extra exercises in the Workbook in a separate section labeled Grammar Booster. The Grammar Booster content is not tested on any *Summit* tests.

UNIT 6

Modals and modal-like expressions: summary

Make polite requests
- **Could** I get your phone number?
- **Can** my son have just one more cookie?
- **Would** you please hold this for a second? (with you only)
- **May** I have a cup of coffee? (formal, with I or we only)

Express preferences
- I **would like to** see that movie.
- **Would** you **like to** go running?
- I'd **rather not** see a movie.
- I **would rather** have left earlier.

Give or ask for permission
- You **can** open the window if you want.
- **Can** I leave this here?
- You **may** leave early if you need to. (formal)
- **May** I leave my coat here? (formal, with I or we only)

Express ability or lack of ability
- He **can** complete the job for you in an hour.
- **Can** you write well in English?
- We **couldn't** finish the report yesterday.
- **Couldn't** you find the restaurant?
- My grandmother **isn't able to** walk any more.
- **Is** she **able to** take care of herself?
- She **was able to** do a lot more when she was younger.

Give a warning
- Your mother **had better** see a doctor right away.
- You **had better not** forget about your appointment.
- He **had better have** called this morning.
- They **had better not have** hurt any animals when they made that movie.

Note: Had better is generally not used in questions. In spoken English, the contraction 'd better is almost always used.

Modals and modal-like expressions: summary (continued)

Express possibility
It **may** rain this afternoon.
He **may not** be able to come this morning.
She **may have** forgotten to lock the door.
She **may not have** remembered.
It **might** be noisy at that restaurant.
She **might not** want to eat anything.
He **might have** gone home already.
He **might not have** paid yet.
It **could** rain tomorrow.
We **could have** paid less.

Draw conclusions
Your father **must** be very smart.
She **must not** think it's important.
They **must have** been exhausted when they got home.
He **must not have** sent it.

Suggest alternatives
You **could** take the next train.

Give suggestions
They really **should** think about staying longer.
He **shouldn't have** waited to make a reservation.
They **should have** called first.
You **shouldn't** stay at that hotel.
They really **ought to** think about staying longer.
They **ought to have** called first.
Should we **have** called first?

Note: Ought to is not usually used in negative statements or questions. Use shouldn't or should instead.

Express necessity
We **have to** take the test tomorrow.
We**'ve got to** arrive on time. [informal, spoken]
All students **must** take the test. [formal]

Express lack of necessity
You **don't have to** have a passport.
She **didn't have to** pay a late fee.

Express prohibition or deny permission
New employees **cannot** (OR **shouldn't**) park their cars in the garage.
New employees **must not** park their cars in the garage. [formal]
New employees **may not** park their cars in the garage. [formal]

Note: In questions, have to is generally used. Questions with must are very formal and not very common. Past necessity is expressed with had to.
Does everyone **have to** take the test?
Must everyone take the test?
All students **had to** take the test.

A Cross out the one modal that *cannot* be used in each sentence or question.

1 (May / Can / Could) your mother please call me tonight?
2 I (wasn't able to / couldn't / shouldn't) get there on time because the traffic was so bad.
3 She (may / had better / can) be able to complete the job by tomorrow.
4 (Can / Should / Ought to) my students listen in while you practice?
5 Shoppers (may / have to / must) not park their cars in front of the main entrance.
6 Thank goodness she (doesn't have to / must not / was able to) renew her passport for another five years.
7 You (could / had better / should) let them know you won't be able to make it on time, or you may not get the job.
8 This restaurant is so good we (ought to / might / would rather) come here more often.

B Circle the one modal that best completes each conversation.

1 A: Why didn't you come to the party last night?
   B: I (had to / have to / must / have got to) study for a test.

2 A: You really (can't / should / mustn't / are able to) call more often.
   B: You're right. I'm sorry.

3 A: She ('d better not have / should have / had to have / must have) forgotten the tickets!
   B: Uh-oh. I hate to tell you this, but I think she did.

4 A: Do you think I ('m able to / must / would / could) get your phone number?
   B: Sure.

5 A: Did you get to go to the movies?
   B: Yeah. But I (must have / 'd rather have / should not have / would have) stayed at home.

6 A: Unfortunately, the doctor (shouldn't / has to / won't be able to / had better) see you until tomorrow.
   B: That's OK. No problem.

7 A: What do you think happened to Judy?
   B: She (must not have / shouldn't have / isn't able to / didn't have to) known we were starting so early.

UNIT 7

The passive voice: review and expansion

Verbs can be transitive or intransitive. A transitive verb can have a direct object. An intransitive verb cannot have a direct object. With an intransitive verb, there can't be a "receiver" of an action.
- Transitive: We **bought** a car. (a car = a direct object)
- Intransitive: We **slept** well. (The verb sleep can't have an object.)

Remember: In the active voice, the subject of a sentence performs the action of the verb. In the passive voice, the subject of the sentence is the receiver of the action of a verb. Form the passive voice with a form of be and a past participle, or with a modal + a form of be and a past participle.

Common intransitive verbs	
arrive	rain
come	seem
die	sit
fall	sleep
go	stand
happen	stay
laugh	walk
live	

Statements

The simple present tense
The ad **is seen** by at least a million people a day.

The simple past tense
At the meeting, people **were called** by their first names.

The present continuous
Every house **is being painted** white.

The future with be going to
Maurizio's new fashions **are going to be shown** on TV tonight.

The future perfect
If I wear this dress before the event, it **will have been seen** by everyone and it won't seem new.

The past continuous
Before we had regulations, dangerous products **were being tested** on small animals.

The present perfect
We**'ve been helped** a lot by our friends.

The past perfect
The aloha shirt **had been worn** only on Fridays for a couple of years before people started wearing them every day.

Modals
Sometimes the truth **can't be** easily **seen**.
My teacher said my essay **should be rewritten** to make it clearer.

Note: The passive voice of the future continuous and the present perfect continuous are rarely used, so they aren't included in this list.

Questions

Invert the subject and the auxiliary verb (the form of be or have) or the modal.
- **Is** Russian **spoken** by many people in Chicago?
- **Has** your uncle **been hired** by an advertising company?
- When **will** she **be given** a new office?
- Who **have** you **been called** by?
- Where **should** we **be married**?
- How **can** this house **be painted** in only two days?

A Write a check mark next to the three sentences that have an intransitive verb.

☐ 1 Valentino's new line of women's purses arrives in stores next week.
☐ 2 Models are wearing very short dresses this season.
☐ 3 My parents are opening a new restaurant downtown.
☐ 4 The owner of the boutique lived in an apartment above the shop.
☐ 5 People speak French in Quebec.
☐ 6 It rained really hard last night.
☐ 7 Advertisers never tell the complete story about defective products.

B On a separate sheet of paper, rewrite in the passive voice the four sentences from Exercise A that have transitive verbs.

C On a separate sheet of paper, rewrite each statement in the passive voice.

1 Joan Saslow and Allen Ascher wrote this book.
2 Students practice English online in most language schools today.
3 Ads can persuade people to buy products.
4 Some ads have manipulated people's emotions.
5 My friend was driving the car when the accident occurred.

D On a separate sheet of paper, rewrite the sentences you wrote for Exercise C as yes / no questions.

E On a separate sheet of paper, write information questions, using the question words and phrases in parentheses.

1 That new shampoo was endorsed by Larissa La Rue. (when)
2 Those beauty products are being manufactured. (where)
3 The car can be bought at the sale price. (for how long)
4 The winner of the election will be known. (what time)
5 The new school was being built. (in what year)

UNIT 8

Making comparisons: review and expansion

Comparative forms of adjectives and adverbs show how two things are different.
- John is **taller than** Rob (is).
- This movie was **less interesting than** the last one (was).
- My sister types **a lot faster than** I (do).

Superlative forms of adjectives and adverbs show how one thing is different from everything else.
- She was **the nicest** person I ever met!
- That was **the least entertaining** movie I ever saw.
- Of all the actors, she sang **the most beautifully**.
- Among my friends, Ned and Stacey definitely have **the most** money.
- Of all the cars we looked at, the Linkus costs **the most**.

Use the determiners **more**, **the most**, **less**, **least**, **little**, **the least**, **fewer**, and **the fewest** with nouns to compare quantities and amounts.
- There is **less** corruption in the government than there used to be.
- I want to be healthy, so I eat **fewer** sweets than **most** people.
- **Few** people went to see *Horror City*, but last night had **the fewest** people in the audience.

Be careful! Use <u>the</u> with a superlative form. However, you can omit <u>the</u> if the superlative is not followed by a noun.
- Which student is **the tallest** OR **tallest**?
- NOT ~~Which is tallest student?~~

Comparisons with <u>as</u> ... <u>as</u> show how two things are alike.
- Tom is just **as tall as** George (is).
- She still sings **as beautifully as** she did when she was young.
- My nephew now weighs **as much as** I do.
- I have **as much money** in the bank **as** I did last year.

Use <u>as</u> ... <u>as</u> with <u>almost</u>, <u>about</u>, and <u>not quite</u> to show how two things are similar, but not equal.
- My nephew weighs **almost as** much **as** I do. [I weigh a bit more.]
- The movie is **about as** long **as** his last one. [But it's a bit shorter.]
- This coat is**n't quite as** expensive **as** it looks. [It's actually cheaper.]

Use <u>as</u> ... <u>as</u> with <u>twice</u>, <u>three times</u>, etc., to show that things are not equal at all.
- A Linkus sedan is about **twice as** expensive **as** a Matsu.
- My new computer is **ten times as** fast **as** my old one.

Note: In informal spoken English, it is more common to say "... as tall as me" instead of the more formal "... as tall as I (am)."

Irregular forms

adjective	adverb	comparative	superlative
good	well	better (than)	the best
bad	badly	worse (than)	the worst
far	far	farther / further (than)	the farthest / furthest

A Read each quoted statement. Then complete each sentence using a comparative, superlative, or comparison with <u>as</u> ... <u>as</u>.

1. "The textbook we are using now is very good. The textbook we were using last year was also very good."
   The textbook we're using now is .... the one we were using last year.

2. "Star shampoo costs about $6.00. Ravel shampoo costs about $7.00. Sanabel shampoo costs about $5.00."
   Among the three shampoos, Sanabel is ....

3. "We paid four hundred euros each for our tickets. They paid three hundred euros."
   We paid .... they did.

4. "Matt has only a little experience working with children. Nancy has a lot of experience."
   Matt has .... Nancy.

5. "John's laptop weighs 2 kilos. Gerry's laptop weighs 2.1 kilos."
   John's laptop isn't .... Gerry's is.

6. "Mark knows only a little Japanese. Jonah knows a lot."
   Mark knows .... Jonah does.

7. "Bart ate a lot for lunch. Susan ate a lot for lunch, too."
   Susan ate .... Bart did for lunch.

Other uses of comparatives, superlatives, and comparisons with <u>as</u> ... <u>as</u>

For emphasis
- The Nile River is **more than** 5,500 kilometers long. [emphasizes that the river is very long]
- The Dickens School now has **fewer than** 900 students. [emphasizes that this is a relatively small number]
- That was **the worst** movie **ever**. [emphasizes that this was a bad movie]
- This meal was **the best of all time**! [emphasizes that this was a great meal]

GRAMMAR BOOSTER

A newborn Asian elephant can weigh **as much as** 150 kilos. [emphasizes that this is fairly heavy]
As many as 200 of these animals are killed every year. [emphasizes that this is a high number]
Milton Academy is **one of the best** schools in the city.
Preet Gupta is **among the most intelligent** commentators on any TV news program today.
The lions in the Central Zoo are **some of the finest** examples of African wildlife you can see without going to Africa.

To show progression
My son is getting **taller** every day. [He's growing.]
The economy is **stronger** now. [It's improving.]

To show tendencies or preferences
We eat out **more than** in. [We tend to eat out.]
Sara likes being alone **more than** socializing. [She prefers to spend time alone.]

To clarify
He's a lot **friendlier than** you would think. [You may think he's not friendly, but in fact he is.]
She's **more of a singer than** a dancer. [People may think she's mainly a dancer, but in fact she's mainly a singer.]
The movie's **more annoying than** scary. [You may think this movie will be scary, but in fact it's just annoying.]
It looks **more like** snow **than** rain. [You may think it's going to rain, but in fact it looks like it's going to snow.]

B Use a comparative, a superlative, or a comparison with <u>as</u> … <u>as</u> to complete each statement so it has a similar meaning to the information in quotes.

1 "Our meal last night was really inexpensive. It only cost 48 euros for the two of us."
Our meal last night cost ……………………… 50 euros.

2 "Our reading club meetings are getting pretty big. On some nights there are thirty students."
Our reading club meetings sometimes have ……………………… students.

3 "I think our teacher is really great!"
Our teacher is ……………………… ever!

4 "The garden you planted last month has become so beautiful!"
Your garden is getting ……………………… every day!

5 "You might think snails would taste strange, but they actually taste quite good."
Snails taste ……………………… you may think.

6 "You may think Kate is shy, but she's actually very talkative."
Kate is ……………………… than you might think.

7 "There were a lot of great new movies this year. *Cool Water* was one of them."
Cool Water was ……………………… new movies this year.

UNIT 9

Perfect modals: short responses

Compare short responses with perfect modals in the active voice and passive voice.

Active voice

Do you think the first inhabitants of the island came from Sweden?

"They **might have**."
"They **must have**."
"They **had to have**."
"They **couldn't have**."

Passive voice

I wonder if the stone was moved by someone.

"It **might have been**."
"It **must have been**."
"It **had to have been**."
"It **couldn't have been**."

Be careful! In a short response to a question (or statement) with a past form of the verb <u>be</u>, always include <u>been</u>.
A: Was the story of the yeti just a joke?
B: It **must have been**. NOT It ~~must have~~.

Respond to each statement or question with a short response, using a perfect modal.

1 **A:** Is it most likely the Nazca Lines were created by humans?
   B: .... (must)

2 **A:** I wonder if the dinosaurs were killed by a meteor, too.
   B: .... (may)

3 **A:** Did Europeans eat potatoes before the discovery of America?
   B: .... (couldn't)

4 **A:** I guess people didn't realize that the carrier pigeon would become extinct.
   B: .... (must not)

5 **A:** The settlers in the western part of the U.S. must have known the buffalo were in danger.
   B: .... (had to)

6 **A:** It must not have been easy to move those huge stones.
   B: .... (can't)

UNIT 10

Be supposed to: expansion

You can also use <u>be supposed to</u> to express a broadly held opinion. It is similar to "Everyone says ... "
   Green tea ice cream **is supposed to taste** really good.
   Their new album **wasn't supposed to be** very good, but I loved it.
   John **was supposed to have been** rude during the dinner, but I just don't believe it.

A On a separate sheet of paper, rewrite each statement, using <u>be supposed to</u>.

Example: They say the new Fernando Meirelles movie is very violent.

> *The new Fernando Meirelles movie is supposed to be very violent.*

1 Everyone thinks our new manager is really nice.
2 Many people believe acupuncture is an effective treatment for pain.
3 I haven't heard Ashley Morgan sing, but they say she has a beautiful voice.
4 I've never had Ethiopian food, but everyone says it's delicious.
5 They say Paulo Coelho's latest novel is his best yet.
6 Everyone says Myanmar is a fascinating place to visit.
7 It's said that corruption is one of the biggest problems in our city right now.

Would: review

Remember: The modal <u>would</u> can be used to talk about the present or future.

For polite requests in the present or future
   Would you please **close** the door?
   Would you **pick up** some milk on your way home?

To express a present or future result of an unreal condition
   She **wouldn't be** so tired if she took a nap.
   I **would go** see them in concert if the ticket prices weren't so astronomical.

The modal <u>would</u> can also be used in the following ways to talk about the past.

To express past repeated or habitual actions
   As children, we **would play** in the park every Saturday.

As the past form of the future with <u>will</u>
   He said he **would get** here before noon. (He said, "I'll get there before noon.")
   She promised she **wouldn't forget**. (She said, "I promise I won't forget.")

To express past intentions or plans that changed
   I thought I **would marry** Harry, but I changed my mind.
   We didn't think we **would enjoy** eating alligator, but it was delicious.

B Write a check mark next to each sentence that expresses a past repeated or habitual action.

☐ 1 I thought we would go skiing in Chile, but we didn't.
☐ 2 In the summer, they would sit outside and read books or just take naps.
☐ 3 I had agreed that I would make breakfast that morning.
☐ 4 Every night, he would lie awake for hours thinking about her.
☐ 5 She warned them that Jake would forget to bring the keys, and she was right.
☐ 6 When Kyle was still living with his parents, he would work on weekdays and study on weekends.
☐ 7 Leila didn't think English would be useful on her trip to Moscow, but she was wrong.
☐ 8 As a student, I would stay up late every night studying for exams.
☐ 9 She asked me if I would help her with her homework that afternoon.
☐ 10 She wouldn't have such a hard time doing her homework if she studied harder.
☐ 11 When I was younger, my dad would always help me with my homework.
☐ 12 I wouldn't go see that new Tom Cruise movie if I were you.
☐ 13 Would you buy an electric car if it were affordable?
☐ 14 My brother thought he would be late.

Grammar for Writing: placement of adverbs of manner

Adverbs of manner modify adjectives or verbs. When they modify adjectives, they go before the adjective.
   The path can be **dangerously** slippery.
   The architecture is **incredibly** beautiful.

When they modify transitive verbs, adverbs of manner ending in -ly often go before the main verb. They can also go after a verb and its direct object.
   She **slowly** opened the door. OR She opened the door **slowly**.
   She should **slowly** open the door. OR She should open the door **slowly**.

When they modify intransitive verbs, adverbs of manner ending in -ly often go after the main verb. They can also go after a verb and an indirect object.
   He spoke **angrily** about corruption. OR He spoke about corruption **angrily**.

Be careful! Don't place adverbs of manner without -ly before a main verb.
   He drives **fast**. NOT He fast drives.
   She can sing really **well**. NOT She can really well sing.

Don't place an adverb of manner between a transitive verb and its direct object.
   He drank his tea **quickly**. OR He **quickly** drank his tea.
      NOT He drank quickly his tea.

Other adverbs of manner
angrily	poorly
badly	quietly
fast	sadly
happily	slowly
hard	softly
nicely	suddenly
noisily	well

C Write a check mark if the adverb is correctly placed. Then, on a separate sheet of paper, rewrite the sentences that you didn't check.

☐ 1 When the game was over, he left quickly the court.
☐ 2 As she drove into town, she sang to herself softly.
☐ 3 The meeting was suddenly postponed after the CEO arrived.
☐ 4 They washed noisily the dishes after dinner.
☐ 5 Tom replied angrily to the text message.
☐ 6 They entered quietly the room and sat in the corner.

D On a separate sheet of paper, rewrite each sentence with one or more adverbs of manner. Choose from the list above and on page 119.

1 I watched the snake until it moved.
2 We chatted until the sun came up the next morning.
3 She speaks Italian, but she doesn't really understand it.
4 He wrote about his experiences living in Cambodia.
5 A cow walked onto the road, and the bus stopped.

SUMMIT 1B

Pronunciation Booster

Pronunciation Booster

The Pronunciation Booster is optional. It provides a pronunciation lesson and practice to support speaking in each unit, making students' speech more comprehensible.

UNIT 6

Sound reduction

In everyday speech, sounds in unstressed words are often "reduced"; that is, vowels change to /ə/ or /ɚ/ or consonants are dropped.

Vowel reduction

The /u/ sound in the function word <u>to</u> is often reduced to /ə/.
  I'll be going **to** the airport after dinner. /tə/
  It's ten **to** two. /tə/

The /æ/ sound in many one-syllable function words is often reduced to /ə/.
  Look **at** that. /ət/
  I saw **an** eagle. /ən/
  That's more **than** I need. /ðən/

Be careful! Function words that occur at the end of a sentence are never reduced.
  What a beautiful bird you **are**! /ɑr/
  What are you looking **at**? /æt/
  What are you waiting **for**? /fɔr/
  Who's she talking **to**? /tu/

The /ɑr/ and /ɔr/ sounds in function words are often reduced to /ɚ/.
  Pets **are** no trouble. /ɚ/
  Is it black **or** white? /ɚ/
  Where's **your** parrot? /yɚ/
  He's been gone **for** days. /fɚ/

The function word <u>and</u> is often reduced to /ən/ when it occurs between two subjects, objects, modifiers, verbs, or phrases.
  They have long arms **and** legs. /ən/
  She laughed **and** cried when she heard the news. /ən/
  We stayed out late **and** went dancing. /ən/

Be careful! The vowel sound /æ/ in <u>and</u> is generally not reduced when it occurs at the beginning of a clause, but the consonant sound /d/ may still be dropped.
  He wore a black suit, **and** she wore a green dress. /æn/

The initial /h/ sound is usually dropped in function words.
  What does ̶h̶e mean? /dʌzi/
  It's in ̶h̶is bag. /ɪnɪz/

A ▶6:14 Listen and practice.

1. I'll be going to the airport after dinner.
2. It's ten to two.
3. Look at that.
4. I saw an eagle.
5. That's more than I need.
6. Pets are no trouble.
7. Is it black or white?
8. Where's your parrot?
9. He's been gone for days.
10. They have long arms and legs.
11. She laughed and cried when she heard the news.
12. We stayed out late and went dancing.
13. He wore a black suit, and she wore a green dress.
14. What does he mean?
15. It's in his bag.

B In the following sentences, circle the words you think will be reduced.

1. Alternatives can be found for medical research on animals.
2. A lot can be done to make conditions better on factory farms.
3. Some animals are raised to be used for medical research.
4. Do we have to ban hunting and bullfighting?

▶6:15 Now practice reading each sentence aloud and listen to check.*

UNIT 7

Vowel sounds /i/ and /ɪ/

The sound /i/ is longer and is formed by tensing the tongue.
The sound /ɪ/ is shorter and formed with the tongue relaxed.

/i/	/ɪ/
leave	live
team	Tim
feel	fill
steal	still
feet	fit

The vowel sound /ɪ/ also appears frequently in unstressed syllables.

pla ces   mar ket   mi nute   wo men

> The vowel sounds /i/ and /ɪ/ are represented in spelling in a number of ways.
>
> | /i/ | /ɪ/ |
> |---|---|
> | steal | blimp |
> | steep | syllable |
> | people | busy |
> | handy | building |
> | believe | women |
> | receive | pretty |
> | boutique | been |
> | key | give |

A ▶6:16 Listen and practice.

1 leave   live
2 team   Tim
3 feel   fill
4 steal   still
5 feet   fit

B ▶6:17 Listen and practice.

1 places   2 market   3 minute   4 women

C ▶6:18 Listen to each pair of words. Circle if they are the <u>same</u> or <u>different</u>.

1 same   different   5 same   different
2 same   different   6 same   different
3 same   different   7 same   different
4 same   different   8 same   different

D ▶6:19 Listen and check which sound you hear in the stressed syllable.

/i/ /ɪ/   /i/ /ɪ/
1 ☐ ☐   8 ☐ ☐
2 ☐ ☐   9 ☐ ☐
3 ☐ ☐   10 ☐ ☐
4 ☐ ☐   11 ☐ ☐
5 ☐ ☐   12 ☐ ☐
6 ☐ ☐   13 ☐ ☐
7 ☐ ☐   14 ☐ ☐

▶6:20 Now listen again and practice.

Stress placement: prefixes and suffixes

Stress placement does not change when most prefixes and suffixes are added to a word.

im**por**tant	unim**por**tant	im**por**tance	im**por**tantly
o**be**dient	o**be**dience	diso**be**dience	o**be**diently
happy	un**hap**py	**hap**piness	**hap**pily

However, adding the suffixes <u>-ion</u>, <u>-ic</u>, <u>-ity</u>, <u>-ical</u>, and <u>-ian</u> generally shifts stress to the syllable before the suffix.

educate → edu**ca**tion
photograph → photo**graph**ic
de**pend**able → dependa**bil**ity
politics → po**lit**ical
music → mu**si**cian

Some nouns and verbs have the same spelling. When the word is a noun, the stress is on the first syllable. When the word is a verb, the stress is on the second syllable.

nouns	verbs
rebel	re**bel**
protest	pro**test**
present	pre**sent**
object	ob**ject**
progress	pro**gress**

Other words in this category
conduct
conflict
contrast
convert
permit
record
survey
suspect

A ▶6:21 Listen and practice.
1 important   unimportant   importance   importantly
2 obedient   obedience   disobedience obediently
3 happy   unhappy   happiness   happily

B ▶6:22 Listen and practice.
1 educate   education
2 photograph photographic
3 dependable dependability
4 politics   political
5 music   musician

C Look at the stressed syllable of each word in Column A. According to the rules given in the chart on page 147, mark the stressed syllable of each word in Column B.

A	B
1 fa ˈmil iar	fa mil ˈiar i ty
2 e ˈmo tion al	e mo ˈtion al ly
3 ˈreg u late	reg u ˈla tion
4 ap ˈpre cia tive	ap ˈpre cia tive ly
5 ˈsym pa thy	sym pa ˈthet ic
6 hy ˈpoth e size	hy po ˈthet i cal
7 ˈbeau ty	ˈbeau ti fy
8 ˈhis to ry	his ˈtor i cal
9 ma ˈte ri al ist	ma te ri al ˈis tic
10 ˈpol i tics	pol i ˈti cian

▶ 6:23 Now practice reading each word aloud and listen to check.*

D ▶ 6:24 Listen and practice.

Nouns	Verbs		Nouns	Verbs
1 rebel	rebel		8 contrast	contrast
2 protest	protest		9 convert	convert
3 present	present		10 permit	permit
4 object	object		11 record	record
5 progress	progress		12 survey	survey
6 conduct	conduct		13 suspect	suspect
7 conflict	conflict			

E Circle the syllable you think will be stressed in each blue word.

1 A summer fishing **permit permits** you to fish all you want.
2 The **protest** was organized to **protest** government spending.
3 All the employees were **surveyed** so the results of the **survey** would be useful.
4 The **contrast** between them now is not great compared to how much they **contrast** at other times of the year.
5 We strongly **object** to the decision to sell art **objects** outside the museum.

▶ 6:25 Now practice reading each sentence aloud, paying attention to words that are both nouns and verbs. Listen to check.*

148 PRONUNCIATION BOOSTER

UNIT 9

Reduction and linking in perfect modals in the passive voice

In perfect modals in the passive voice, the modal and the auxiliary verbs <u>have been</u> are said together as one unit. Note that stress falls on the modal and the main verb. In everyday speech, the /h/ sound in the auxilliary <u>have</u> is dropped and /æ/ is reduced to /ə/.

/ˈkʊdəvbɪn/
They **COULD have been** KILLED.

/ˈmaitəvbɪn/
They **MIGHT have been** LOST.

/ˈmʌstəvbɪn/
They **MUST have been** MOVED.

/ˈmeiyəvbɪn/
They **MAY have been** DISCOVERED.

With <u>had to</u>, stress <u>had</u> and the main verb. Say <u>had to</u> and <u>have been</u> as one unit.

/ˈhætuəvbɪn/
They **HAD to have been** STOLEN.

In negative perfect modals, stress falls on the modal, the word <u>not</u>, and the main verb. In everyday speech, <u>not</u> and the auxiliary verbs <u>have been</u> are generally said as one unit.

/ˈnatəvbɪn/
They **MIGHT NOT have been** LOST.
They **MUST NOT have been** MOVED.

A ▶6:26 Listen and practice.

1. They could have been killed.
2. They might have been lost.
3. They must have been moved.
4. They may have been discovered.
5. They had to have been stolen.
6. They might not have been lost.
7. They must not have been moved.

B Underline where you think the words should be linked and which sounds should be reduced.

1. The damage may have been caused by a storm.
2. The building could have been destroyed by a fire.
3. The gold figures couldn't have been stolen.
4. The stone statues must have been moved using animals.
5. The drawings must not have been discovered until later.
6. The islands had to have been inhabited by Polynesians.
7. The secrets of Rapa Nui might not have been lost.

▶6:27 Now practice reading each sentence aloud, paying attention to reductions. Listen to check.*

Vowel sounds /eɪ/, /ɛ/, /æ/, and /ʌ/

The sound /eɪ/ is longer and is formed by tensing the tongue with the lips spread.
The sounds /ɛ/, /æ/, and /ʌ/ are shorter and are formed with the tongue relaxed.
Say /eɪ/ and /ɛ/ with the lips spread wide. Say /æ/ with the lips spread slightly and the mouth slightly open. Say /ʌ/ with the tongue and jaw completely relaxed.

/eɪ/	/ɛ/	/æ/	/ʌ/
pain	pen	pan	pun
Dane	den	Dan	done
mate	met	mat	mutt
bait	bet	bat	but

Mouth positions for vowels
tongue tensed (long)   /eɪ/
tongue relaxed (short)   /ɛ/, /æ/, /ʌ/
lips spread   /eɪ/, /ɛ/, /æ/
jaw relaxed   /ʌ/

The vowel sounds /eɪ/, /ɛ/, /æ/, and /ʌ/ may be represented by these spellings.

/eɪ/	/ɛ/	/æ/	/ʌ/
pay	rest	snacks	up
weigh	sweat	have	some
shape	says	laugh	touch
wait	said	half	does
taking	friend	guarantee	blood
great	guess	relax	what

A ▶6:28 Listen and practice.

1 pain   pen   pan   pun
2 Dane   den   Dan   done
3 mate   met   mat   mutt
4 bait   bet   bat   but

B ▶6:29 Listen to each word and place it in the correct column.

| age | any | just | banned | debt | love | edge | face | flashy | great | health |
| jump | can't | some | faint | enough | chance | text | nothing | trait | way |

/eɪ/	/ɛ/	/æ/	/ʌ/

▶6:30 Now practice reading each word aloud and listen again to check.*

C ▶6:31 Listen to each sentence and circle the word you hear.

1 Give the money to the (men / man).
2 I think it's (Dan / done).
3 What is that (rag / rug) made of?
4 Do you need this (pen / pan)?
5 He's a perfect (mutt / mate).
6 My (date / debt) is causing me trouble.
7 Could you take that (bug / bag) off the counter?
8 Please put a bandage on the (cut / cat).

Now practice reading the sentences both ways.

SUMMIT 1B
Test-Taking Skills Booster

Test-Taking Skills Booster

The Test-Taking Skills Booster is optional. It provides practice in applying some key logical thinking and comprehension skills typically included in reading and listening tasks on standardized proficiency tests. Each unit contains one Reading Completion activity and one or more Listening Completion activities.

The reading selections in the Booster are either adaptations of those from the *Summit 1* units or new reading selections about a related topic. Listening Completion exercises are based on the listening passages that can be found on the audio from the *Summit* units. None of the Reading Completion or Listening Completion tasks duplicate what students have already done in the unit.

*Note that the practice activities in the Booster are not intended to test student achievement after each unit. Complete Achievement Tests for *Summit* can be found in the *Summit* ActiveTeach.

READING COMPLETION
Read the selection. Choose the word or phrase that best completes each statement.

Saving the American Buffalo

One remarkable conservation story is the sustained effort to save the American buffalo, ... was successfully brought back from near extinction. .... the arrival of European settlers in North America, there were more than 50 million buffalo roaming in huge herds across the continent's central flatlands, which are today known as the Great Plains. For Native Americans living on the plains, these magnificent creatures .... food as well as clothing and shelter. The buffalo played an enormously important .... in the plains ecosystem, sustaining other animals and plants on the plains. For example, weaker buffalo provided food for predators such as bears and wolves. Buffalo attracted birds that picked at their fur for insects. And thousands of hooves walking over the landscape kept aggressive plants .... control.

.... , as new settlers moved from the East to settle the West, whole herds were slaughtered, often just for sport. Buffalo were considered an obstacle to the settlers' desire to grow crops and raise cattle. .... , the resource that had sustained Native Americans for centuries began to disappear. By the end of the 1800s, there were as few as 750 buffalo remaining. Many people were shocked that the buffalo, long considered a symbol of the West, had been allowed to come so close to extinction. Fortunately, ... efforts to save them were begun in 1905. The remaining herds were gathered together and protected. As a result, steady .... was made, increasing their numbers to today's population of about 350,000. What conclusion can we draw from this story? It illustrates that conservation efforts can make a difference if they are begun early enough.

1	A which	B even though	C now that	D so that
2	A While	B Because	C Before	D In fact
3	A provided	B took	C made	D sold
4	A species	B character	C role	D place
5	A as	B over	C out of	D under
6	A To sum up	B Secondly	C In summary	D Unfortunately
7	A In contrast	B Consequently	C Similarly	D Still
8	A environment	B ecology	C habitat	D conservation
9	A progress	B reduction	C conservation	D distance

LISTENING COMPLETION

▶ 6:40 You will hear part of a lecture. Read the paragraph below. Then listen and complete each statement with the word or short phrase you hear in the lecture. Listen a second time to check your work.

The lecturer says that most species can be placed into one of two (1) .... : predator or prey. However, she points out that many animals play (2) .... in nature, as predator and prey. She further explains that animals that are prey rely on (3) .... in order to protect themselves from predators. As an example, she points out that fish swim in huge (4) .... in which they move as if the group were one (5) .... This behavior (6) .... predators, causing them to only eat the fish that are outside the group. The lecturer further points out that predators also often travel in groups called (7) .... in order to make it easier to hunt their prey and ensure their own (8) .... She notes that (9) .... in a group makes it possible to kill (10) .... animals.

READING COMPLETION

Read the selection. Choose the word or phrase that best completes each statement.

Compulsive Shopping: the Problem and the Solution

In the last hundred years, the way in which we consume material goods has changed radically. ……………, 1 for our grandparents, shopping was for buying things that were necessary to satisfy physical needs. Today, ……………, 2 although we continue to buy necessities, we now …………… 3 additionally to indulge ourselves in luxuries, such as expensive gym shoes or the latest electronic and digital technology. ……………, 4 shopping itself has for many of us become entertainment. While there is no harm in being entertained, some people have unfortunately gone entirely overboard. …………… 5 for most people an occasional indulgence may cause them to come up a bit short at the end of the month, for others spending becomes a catastrophe with extremely troubling consequences. Such people cannot resist temptation, and they often buy merely to acquire. Then …………… 6 do they find themselves in considerable debt, but they sink into psychological distress …………… 7. Recent studies suggest that extreme impulse buying is on the increase, affecting an estimated 5 to 10 percent of the adult population in many countries. ……………, 8 what can or should be done about this growing worldwide problem? Some say that …………… 9 compulsive shoppers shop to avoid or hide their feelings of anxiety or loneliness, the only way to combat the problem is with psychological counseling and self-awareness. …………… 10 experts, problem shoppers need to learn that "you can't buy happiness."

1	A Likewise	B To begin with	C Secondly	D Similarly
2	A whereas	B furthermore	C in contrast	D following that
3	A entertain	B travel	C work	D shop
4	A Third	B Least importantly	C Secondly	D Even though
5	A Because	B When	C Finally	D Whereas
6	A while	B furthermore	C not only	D in addition
7	A since	B as well	C didn't either	D however
8	A Finally	B For instance	C Therefore	D For one thing
9	A yet	B because	C like	D however
10	A According to	B Whereas	C In contrast to	D Not only

LISTENING COMPLETION

▶ 6:41 You will hear two conversations. Read each paragraph. Then listen and complete each statement with the word or short phrase you hear. Listen a second time to check your work.

Nina greets Ross in the store and he asks her what she's (1) ………………. She tells him that she needs (2) ……………… for her (3) ……………… because her old one is (4) ………………. She has been told that the store has some really (5) ……………… ones. If she can find one with a good price she might buy one for her (6) ……………… too because their air conditioner is really old.

The woman sees a (7) ……………… that she really likes. Her husband agrees that it's (8) ………………, but he wonders if it's (9) ……………… since it has no price tag on it. The wife guesses that the store purposely doesn't put the price on items in the window so customers have to (10) ……………… and ask. The husband says stores like it when customers do that because then if you don't buy the item, they might be able to talk you into (11) ………………. They're happy they (12) ……………… one.

READING COMPLETION
Read the selection. Choose the word or phrase that best completes each statement.

The Consequences of an Aging Population

For the first time in history, we soon will have more .... people than children. However, even more important than the ratio of old to young people is the increase in their actual numbers .... an increase in life expectancy. .... the population of older people gets larger, there will be more cases of age-related conditions and diseases .... , there will be increased needs for medications and equipment. .... , some of the most elderly patients will eventually need constant care and assistance with their most basic activities of daily living, ... more nursing homes will need to be built and more caregivers will have to be trained. .... governmental resources may not be able to cover costs, much of the expense will need to be borne by families and .... institutions.

.... the economic consequences of the growth in the elderly population, there will be significant cultural and social consequences as well. .... in the past it was common for adult children to stay home to care for older relatives, fewer adults are able or willing to take on that role today. .... , the shift to institutional rather than home care will represent an immense social change, especially in cultures where older and younger generations have traditionally lived together.

1	A elderly	B young	C married	D unhappy
2	A because	B due to	C until	D nevertheless
3	A In conclusion	B Whereas	C As	D For example
4	A as well	B either	C yet	D not either
5	A Because	B Since	C While	D Consequently
6	A Even though	B Nevertheless	C First of all	D Furthermore
7	A for instance	B so	C whereas	D yet
8	A Nevertheless	B Because	C All the same,	D Therefore
9	A educational	B sporting	C technical	D charitable
10	A Furthermore	B While	C In addition to	D Unlike
11	A Whenever	B So	C Yet	D While
12	A As a result	B Even though	C First of all	D It's possible

LISTENING COMPLETION

▶ 6:42 You will hear a conversation. Read the paragraph below. Then listen and complete each statement with the word or short phrase you hear in the conversation. Listen a second time to check your work.

A father and his daughter are discussing her (1) .... The father doesn't like the boy because he thinks he's (2) .... He explains by saying that the boyfriend is always (3) .... The daughter complains that her father doesn't have any (4) .... for her (5) .... She tells him that just because he's (6) .... doesn't mean he knows everything. The father gets angry at her tone of voice and tells her (7) .... Now she won't be able to see any movies or make any (8) .... for two weeks!

READING COMPLETION

Read the selection. Choose the word or phrase that best completes each statement.

The Roswell Incident

.... pilot Kenneth Arnold was flying a plane in the northwest of the U.S. on June 25th, 1947, he saw
something strange: objects that looked like plates, or saucers, flying across the sky like a small flock of birds.
His story led to numerous other news stories in which people claimed to have seen similar unidentified flying
objects (UFOs)—or "flying saucers." Shortly after, on July 8th, a secret military balloon crashed near Roswell,
New Mexico, in the southwest. Nevertheless, the local newspaper reported .... that a flying saucer
had crashed, and the news media from all over demanded more information. However, because the balloon
was a secret, the military .... an official story: that the object that had crashed was just an ordinary
weather balloon.

No one questioned that story for more than thirty years. Then, in 1978, UFO lecturer Stanton Friedman
interviewed a man who .... he had seen something stranger than a weather balloon in the wreckage
of the 1947 crash. .... the story of a flying saucer was reborn. Even though versions of that story
..............., most people who believe there was a military conspiracy to hide the truth agree on this basic
detail: a flying saucer crashed near Roswell in 1947. .... the military didn't want anyone to know the
truth, it kept the incident top secret and continues to do so today. Because many details have been added
to the story over the years, many still .... there was a military cover-up. ...., the story has
become a part of popular culture, and Roswell conspiracy fans meet at annual conferences to debate the
various versions.

1 A If   B Because   C While   D Whenever
2 A instead   B likewise   C also   D besides
3 A turned on   B began   C opened   D invented
4 A insisted   B forgot   C questioned   D told
5 A Yet   B But   C So   D Likewise
6 A different   B vary   C agree   D interest
7 A Since   B While   C If   D Despite that
8 A forget   B remember   C believe   D wonder
9 A Despite that B Similarly   C As a result D Even if

LISTENING COMPLETION

▶ 6:43 You will hear a description. Read the paragraph below. Then listen and complete each statement
with the word or short phrase you heard. Listen a second time to check your work.

It is believed that the people of Easter Island may have used the stone figures to (1) .... religious and
political (2) .... and (3) .... In total, 540 figures were moved (4) .... the island.
They may have (5) " .... " the figures to their final destination by using (6) .... to rock the
figures back and forth. It's also possible that they were laid down flat and rolled on logs. However, moving the figures
either way couldn't have been (7) .... with fewer than 70 people. Explorer Thor Heyerdahl believed the
island might have been (8) .... by South Americans. He sailed a raft called the Kon-Tiki in order to
(9) .... that his theory was possible. Ultimately, DNA evidence (10) .... that the original
inhabitants must have come from Polynesia.

160   TEST-TAKING SKILLS BOOSTER

UNIT 10

READING COMPLETION
Read the selection. Choose the word or phrase that best completes each statement.

When You Never Switch Off

In the next few days, ... you find yourself in a public place, look around. Odds are you'll see a large percentage of people on their phones or tablets texting, chatting, checking messages, or surfing the net. We're more connected to our mobile devices .... we have ever been before.

Our devices even follow us into our bedrooms, ... we use all this technology as a means to unwind at the end of a long day. According to a recent poll, a majority of respondents said they use their devices right before going to sleep. Most also reported that using their devices .... keeps them up at night but prevents them from getting enough sleep. Zack Panatera, a student at Stanford University, complained, "I'll take a quick look at something interesting and, the next thing I know, I've spent a few hours online."

.... some experts, the light from an electronic device can throw off our normal sleep cycle. Therefore, they .... people to switch off any kind of technology at least an hour before going to bed.

While lack of sleep may not seem so important, the .... can be huge: one's performance the next day may be affected and it may be harder to pay attention or remember things. .... , technology is a contributing factor in a growing trend toward longer hours at work and less time off. Even though we have left the office, we continue to stay connected. We are .... our work world to enter our private lives in ways that never would have been imaginable in the past.

1	A whereas	B if	C even if	D if only
2	A where	B and	C than	D since
3	A where	B which	C that	D even if
4	A not only	B neither	C either	D but
5	A Due to	B Accordingly	C To illustrate	D According to
6	A advise	B suggest	C recommend	D report
7	A technology	B concern	C consequences	D symptoms
8	A Moreover	B Still	C Otherwise	D In contrast
9	A stopping	B allowing	C telling	D preventing

LISTENING COMPLETION

▶ 6:44 You will hear a speaker. Read the paragraph below. Then listen and complete each statement with the word or short phrase you hear. Listen a second time to check your work.

The speaker points out a (1) .... toward longer hours at work and less time off. People seem to be (2) .... their work world into their (3) .... in ways that weren't (4) .... in the past. Even in people's (5) .... time, technology has reduced face-to-face human (6) .... Instead of going out with others, people are (7) .... at home and (8) .... online. And communication with family, friends, and colleagues—now mainly online—is shorter and more (9) .... than it was in the past. At the end, the lecturer also claims that face-to-face family time is (10) ....

THIRD EDITION

SUMMIT 1B

WORKBOOK

JOAN SASLOW
ALLEN ASCHER

UNIT 6 Animals

PREVIEW

1 Complete the conversations with phrases from the box.

cooped up	in charge	put you in your place
feel sorry for	put up with	

1. **A:** I _____ the animals at the pet store.
   B: Why?
   A: They're _____ in the store all day.
   B: I know. But hopefully they'll find good homes soon.

2. **A:** The neighbor's dog is driving me crazy.
   B: Why? What's it doing?
   A: It barks all night. I can't _____ it any longer.

3. **A:** I tried to give Sara some advice on caring for her parrot, but she told me to mind my own business.
   B: Oh. I guess she _____.

4. **A:** How do your kids like the new puppy?
   B: They love him! But he needs to be trained; he doesn't obey us yet.
   A: Yes, you need to let him know that you're _____.

2 Match each animal with the adjective that best describes it. Write the letter on the line.

a. strong
b. quiet
c. brave
d. hairy
e. blind
f. slow
g. fat
h. cute

 1. _____ a bat

 2. _____ an ox

 3. _____ a mouse

 4. _____ a kitten

 5. _____ a lion

 6. _____ a pig

 7. _____ a gorilla

 8. _____ a snail

W55

3 A simile is an expression that compares two things, using the words <u>like</u> or <u>as</u>. Use your answers from Exercise 2 to write animal similes with <u>as</u>.

1. _as blind as a bat_
2. _____
3. _____
4. _____
5. _____
6. _____
7. _____
8. _____

4 Complete the sentence about yourself with a simile.

I'm _____.

Now use some of the similes from Exercise 3 to describe people you know, famous people, or fictional characters.

1. _My boss is as blind as a bat._
2. _____
3. _____
4. _____
5. _____

LESSON 1

5 Complete the sentences in the passive voice with <u>should</u> and a verb from the box. Some verbs will be used more than once.

allow	give	keep	protect	provide	treat

1. Animals on large farms _____ humanely.
2. They _____ with healthy food.
3. They _____ with clean drinking water.
4. They _____ to interact with other animals.
5. The animals _____ space to move around.
6. They _____ from predators.
7. They _____ for illness or injury.
8. They _____ comfortable in extreme weather.

6 Complete the sentences with passive modals.

1. Dogfighting is illegal in all fifty U.S. states. Dogs _____ for fighting in the United States.
   (can't / raise)

2. Animals _____ for sport or entertainment. Hunting, animal fighting,
   (shouldn't / harm)
   animal racing, and use of animals in circuses should be illegal in all countries.

3. Animals _____ (don't have to / kill) for their hides and fur. It's not necessary, because there are so many man-made materials that can keep people just as warm.

4. The cruel practice of testing cosmetics on animals _____ (can / eliminate) if everyone buys only from companies that don't test on animals.

5. Pets _____ (might not / mistreat) if there were more laws protecting them.

6. Alternatives to animal testing _____ (might / develop) in the next decade.

7 What can be done to promote the humane treatment of animals? List some ideas.

_____

_____

LESSON 2

8 **READING** Read about the advantages and disadvantages of owning different popular pets.

FINDING THE BEST PET FOR YOU
Take time to learn about the animal of your choice before bringing one home.

CATS

Cats are independent and easy pets to care for. And, as long as you aren't buying a purebred, they are economical pets, too.

Cats require little actual day-to-day care. They clean and groom themselves, tend to be self-reliant, and are usually happy to stay out of your way. But they can also be cuddly, playful, affectionate creatures—when they are interested.

Finding a kitten is usually easy, and they are often free.

DOGS

Dogs are generally eager to please, affectionate, loyal, and protective, but they demand lots of time and attention. They need plenty of exercise and thrive on interaction with their owners. Daily walks, frequent baths, and feeding are a must.

Dogs range in price from free to quite expensive for some breeds. If you decide to buy a purebred, research the various dog breeds to find the best match for your particular household.

RABBITS

Rabbits love to run, are very sociable and intelligent, and most are quite adorable.

When deciding whether a rabbit is the pet for you, keep in mind that they require daily attention and care, much like dogs. A rabbit should get lots of exercise, live in a dry spot in your home, and get time out of its cage.

Rabbits are not costly to purchase or care for, though it's important to keep fresh hay and leafy greens on hand for them to eat.

(continued on page 58)

Finding the Best Pet for You *(continued)*

HAMPSTERS	Hamsters are easy pets for practically any family. They are amusing, affable, and cute. Hamsters have simple needs and are cheap to buy and to keep. Provide a dry living space outfitted with a gnawing log and a hiding place, and a hamster is content.	
BIRDS 	Birds have been blessed with lovely voices, though they are not quiet pets. Despite this, they are intelligent companions that are growing in popularity because they are pretty and quite independent. Caring for birds is not difficult, but they do have special needs. They like to be active and to be challenged, and they must be housed in a place that is not too hot or too cold. Most love human interaction or other bird companions. They should all be released from their cages periodically to explore their surroundings and to have the opportunity to fly. Birds can be quite costly to purchase, depending on which bird you buy, but the cost of caring for a bird is quite low.	
SNAKES	If you're the average person, this is not the pet you want. Snakes require careful attention and owners with special knowledge to care for them. Before you buy a snake, consider that it may grow up to weigh twice what you do and refuse to eat anything but live animals such as mice or insects, which you will need to provide. Temperature and lighting must be controlled, and the snake's enclosure must be secure. Snakes range from being placid and docile to aggressive, depending on the individual snake. They can be fairly costly to purchase and to maintain.	
FISH	Fish fit well in almost any type of household. They're quiet, generally peaceful, and, depending on your tastes, not expensive to buy or to shelter. Care is relatively simple and involves monitoring water and food. Usually, the biggest expense involves an aquarium, some of which can be very expensive. For those who do not want exotic, pricey fish, a simple, adequately built aquarium will do and costs much less.	

Now complete the chart with information from the reading.

Pet	Personality traits	Care / special needs	Cost
Cats	independent, self-reliant	easy to care for	economical, often free
Dogs			
Rabbits			
Hamsters			
Birds			
Snakes			
Fish			

9 Use information from the chart in Exercise 8 to answer the following questions.

> Researchers have documented many health benefits associated with pet ownership. Owning a pet can help:
> - reduce stress
> - relieve loneliness and depression
> - lower blood pressure
> - prevent heart disease
> - lower health-care costs
> - stimulate exercise
> - encourage laughter
> - facilitate social contact

1. Which pets are low-maintenance?
   _____

2. Which pets are high-maintenance?
   _____

3. Which pets are costly to buy or care for?
   _____

4. Which pets are inexpensive to buy or care for?
   _____

5. Which pet would be best for your lifestyle? Explain.
   _____
   _____

Small dog breeds have become trendy in recent years. Celebrities such as Jessica Simpson and Lindsay Lohan are often spotted with their toy dogs tucked in their purses. As a result of this popularity, designer labels are selling high-end products for dogs—including clothes, collars, and jewelry.

LESSON 3

10 Complete the diagram to give examples of <u>Predators</u> and <u>Prey</u>. Use some animals from Student's Book page 62 and other animals that you know. List animals that can be both Predators and Prey where the circles overlap.

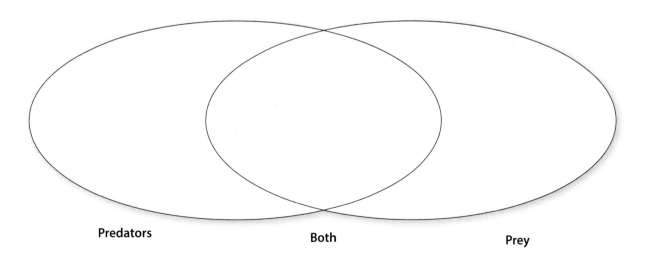

Predators   Both   Prey

Animals   W59

11 Write sentences about three of the animals you listed in Exercise 10. What are their physical features? Do they form social groups? How do they hunt if they are predators? If they are prey, what do they do to protect themselves when they are threatened?

_____
_____
_____
_____
_____
_____

12 Look at the photos. What is each animal doing? Can you think of a similar human behavior? Complete the chart.

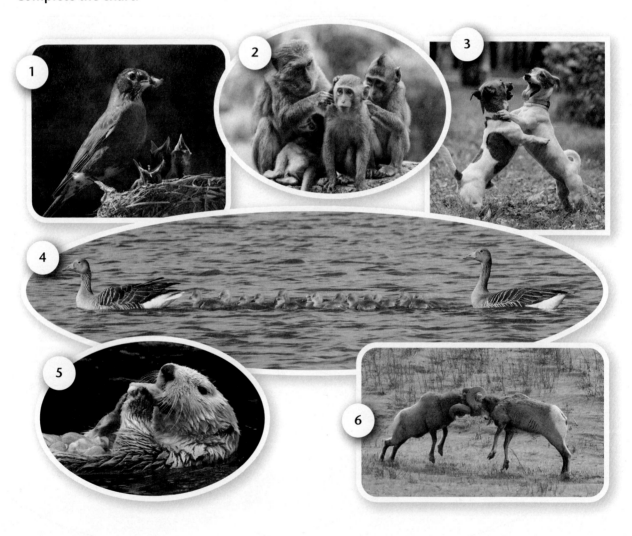

Animal behavior	Human behavior
1. Birds catch bugs and worms for their babies, bring them back to the nest, and feed the babies by putting the food in their beaks.	Humans make food for their babies and feed them with a bottle or a spoon.
2.	
3.	
4.	
5.	
6.	

13 **CHALLENGE** Expressions about animals are sometimes used to describe human behavior. Complete each expression with the correct animal.

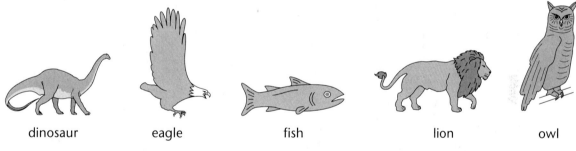

dinosaur   eagle   fish   lion   owl

1. To feel like a _____ **out of water** is to feel uncomfortable because you are in an uncomfortable place or situation.
2. Someone who is _____ **-eyed** is very good at seeing or noticing things.
3. A **night** _____ is someone who enjoys staying awake late at night.
4. Someone who is brave is _____ **hearted**.
5. Something large and old-fashioned that doesn't work well anymore is a _____.

14 Write your own sentences, using three of the animal expressions from Exercise 13.

Example: <u>I would feel like a fish out of water if I moved to the country.</u>

1. _____
2. _____
3. _____

LESSON 4

15 READING Read the article.

The Death of a Lion Ignites Trophy Hunting Debate

In the summer of 2015, American dentist Walter Palmer went into hiding. Thousands of angry strangers were sending him and his family threatening messages via social media. Protestors appeared outside his office and home, waving signs calling him an evil murderer. What did Palmer do to set off this firestorm of negative attention? He went trophy hunting.

More specifically, Palmer participated in a hunting trip in the African country of Zimbabwe, during which he killed a lion. At the time, Palmer was unaware that the lion was a popular attraction at the nearby Hwange National Park, a protected game reserve. Nicknamed "Cecil," the 13-year-old lion was beloved by tourists for its unusual black mane and camera-friendly personality. Palmer also didn't know that Cecil was the subject of a 9-year wildlife conservation study run by Oxford University and wore a GPS collar that tracked its movements. Palmer, an avid big game hunter, spent $54,000 to hire local professional guides and to obtain a government hunting permit. After the guides illegally lured the lion out of the national park and onto private land, Palmer killed it, keeping the head and skin as a trophy. When news spread of Cecil's death, animal lovers across the world were outraged. The ethics of trophy hunting became a source of intense international debate.

Advocates insist that trophy hunting can bring long-term benefits for wildlife. For example, it's estimated that sport hunters spend over 2.9 billion dollars every year on permits and fees. This revenue can be used to fund conservation programs, establish national parks, and fight poachers who kill endangered animals illegally. Supporters also argue that the promise of income from hunters can motivate local landowners to support, rather than kill, endangered wildlife. When South Africa legalized the hunting of white rhinos, landowners reintroduced the species onto their properties, helping to increase the population from fewer than 100 to more than 11,000. Hunters also point out that they target only the largest animals—often males that are too old to reproduce. Removing these aggressive senior males can give younger males more access to the females, and more opportunities for the population to grow.

However, opponents of trophy hunting dispute these claims, arguing that little of the revenue generated by hunting is actually used for conservation. Rather, the money often disappears into the pockets of corrupt government officials. Critics also point out that responsible nature tourism generates significantly more revenue than trophy hunting. Studies from nine African countries show that hunting amounts to less than 2% of the total tourism revenue, a fact which clearly illustrates that tourists visit African countries to see and photograph wildlife, not kill it.

Furthermore, these reports estimate that only 3% of hunting revenue actually makes it back to the local communities where the hunting takes place. Finally, many animal lovers believe that it is our responsibility to protect endangered wildlife and that it's unethical to allow rich hunters to kill rare and beautiful animals for sport.

While Walter Palmer claims to regret killing Cecil the lion, it's clear that trophy hunting has become a controversial issue. Do we need to kill animals in order to save them? With strong opinions on both sides, the debate will likely continue.

Now answer the questions.

1. Why were people so angry at Walter Palmer? _____

2. What was special about Cecil? _____

3. What did Palmer's guides do that was illegal? _____

4. What effect did Palmer's actions have worldwide? _____

5. According to the supporters of trophy hunting, how does hunting benefit animal conservation? _____

6. What arguments do trophy hunting opponents make against the benefits you listed in item 5? _____

16 **WHAT DO YOU THINK? Answer the questions.**

1. Who do you think is more to blame for the killing of Cecil, a protected animal—Walter Palmer, or his guides? Explain your answer. _____

2. What is your opinion of the reactions to Palmer on social media? Were the reactions justified? _____

3. What is your opinion on trophy hunting? Which arguments from the article do you find most convincing? _____

> According to many scientists, thousands of plant and animal species are at risk of extinction in the next few decades. One in three amphibians and a fifth of all mammals are threatened. Also, 68 percent of all plants are at risk of extinction.

GRAMMAR BOOSTER

A Choose the modal that best completes each sentence.

1. I _____ have a pet parrot, but they require too much care.
   a. had better   b. would like to   c. am able to   d. should

2. If you don't mind, I _____ eat out tonight.
   a. wouldn't   b. don't have to   c. would rather not   d. must not

3. _____ Hillary play the violin well?
   a. Should   b. Must   c. May   d. Can

4. I'm sorry, but I _____ come to the meeting tomorrow.
   a. must not   b. won't be able to   c. couldn't   d. don't have to

5. Your sister's a tennis player? She _____ be very athletic.
   a. must   b. could   c. should   d. may

6. We _____ go skiing this weekend. We haven't decided yet.
   a. shouldn't   b. can't   c. had better not   d. might not

7. You _____ feed the animals—it's against the rules!
   a. don't have to   b. might not   c. had better not   d. aren't able to

8. I _____ take this class. It's required.
   a. may   b. could   c. have to   d. can

B Complete each sentence with a modal. More than one answer may be possible.

1. You _____ turn on the TV while you wait, if you'd like.
2. It _____ snow tomorrow.
3. _____ I please borrow your pen for a moment?
4. If we leave at 4:00, there _____ be a lot of traffic.
5. We _____ check the weather before we go hiking.
6. If you don't want to see a movie, we _____ go out to eat instead.
7. My mother-in-law _____ have liked to go to Ireland, but she went to France instead.
8. He _____ have been very happy when he found out about his promotion.
9. You _____ smoke in this restaurant; it's prohibited.
10. He _____ come to the party last night because he had to work.

C   Complete each conversation in your own way. Use a modal.

1. **A:** I passed Ellie on the street yesterday, and she didn't say hello.
   B: *She may not have seen you.*

2. **A:** It's too warm in here.
   B: _____

3. **A:** I don't feel like cooking tonight.
   B: _____

4. **A:** I don't know where to go on vacation this year.
   B: _____

5. **A:** Class was canceled yesterday.
   B: _____

6. **A:** I've had this cold for three weeks now.
   B: _____

7. **A:** I'm a little hungry.
   B: _____

8. **A:** My brother wants to get a pet.
   B: _____

WRITING: Supporting a point of view

A **PREWRITING: PLANNING YOUR ARGUMENT** Read the question below. State your opinion and list your arguments. Try to include examples, facts, or experts' opinions to support your opinion. Then list possible opposing arguments.

Is animal conservation important?

Your opinion: _____

Your arguments	Possible opposing arguments
1. _____	1. _____
2. _____	2. _____
3. _____	3. _____

B **WRITING** Write a paragraph arguing your opinion from Exercise A. Remember to include a topic sentence at the beginning of the paragraph and a concluding sentence at the end.

_____
_____
_____
_____
_____
_____
_____
_____
_____
_____
_____
_____

C **SELF-CHECK**
☐ Did I state my point of view clearly in the introduction?
☐ Did I provide examples, facts, or experts' opinions to support my point of view?
☐ Did I discuss opposing arguments?
☐ Did I include a concluding sentence?

UNIT 7

Advertising and Consumers

PREVIEW

1 Read the social media posts about shopping mistakes.

> We all make shopping mistakes once in a while. Are there any mistakes that you make regularly?
>
> View 4 more comments
>
> **Tia Marks**
> I'm a sucker for ads with celebrities in them. If I see a photo of a famous actress in a particular brand of clothing or makeup, then I suddenly want the same thing! It's crazy, I know. And expensive!
> Like • Reply • 1 hr 53 mins
>
> **Adam Baker**
> I guess you could say my problem is "keeping up with the Joneses." What I mean is this: If one of my friends gets a new phone or gadget, I feel like I need to go out and get one that's just as good or even better.
> Like • Reply • 1 hr 47 mins
>
> **Sandra Drummond**
> I can't pass up a good sale. There's something about getting a good deal, even if I don't need the product that's on sale. For example, last week a local store had a sale on backpacks, so I bought one. It's a really good backpack, and I got it for half price, but I don't need a backpack!
> Like • Reply • 1 hr 32 mins
>
> **Alex Smith**
> My problem is Internet shopping. It's so easy. When I'm bored, I start surfing the net, and often I end up buying something. And it's usually something I don't really need.
> Like • Reply • 1 hr 14 mins

Now describe each person's problem in your own words and write advice for each person.

1. Tia's problem: _____

   Your advice: _____

2. Adam's problem: _____

   Your advice: _____

3. Sandra's problem: _____

   Your advice: _____

4. Alex's problem: _____

   Your advice: _____

2 Complete the conversations with phrases from the box.

Don't fall for that.	Tell you what.
I could kick myself.	We'll call it even.
I owe you one.	You're comparing apples and oranges.

1. **A:** _____
   B: Why? What happened?

2. **A:** Look at this makeup. They say it will remove wrinkles!
   B: _____ There's no way that can be true.

3. **A:** My cat is much easier to take care of than my dog.
   B: They're very different types of pets. _____

4. **A:** I don't know if I can finish this report by the end of the day.
   B: _____ I don't have too much to do today. I'll lend you a hand.
   A: Thanks! _____

5. **A:** Thanks for helping me with my computer. How can I repay you?
   B: Oh, you've helped me many times. _____

LESSON 1

3 Read each statement and then suggest the best place for each person to shop in your city or town. Use the vocabulary from Student's Book page 76.

I want to pick up some cheap sunglasses. It would be a waste of money to buy designer ones. I'd just lose them!

1. <u>The open-air market on Fifth Street is a good place for bargain hunting.</u>

I'd like to get some coffee, take a walk in this beautiful weather, and check out the new fall fashions.

2. _____

I've been saving up for a new digital camera. I'd like to check out a couple of different places before I buy one.

3. _____

I don't really need anything, but I wouldn't mind just looking around. I actually find shopping relaxing.

4. _____

4 Look online for something you're interested in buying. Record the prices you find on different websites. Comment on shipping costs, available brands, customer service, etc.

What are you shopping for? _____

Any particular brand? _____

Website: _____
Price: _____
Comments: _____
_____

Website: _____
Price: _____
Comments: _____
_____

Website: _____
Price: _____
Comments: _____
_____

Which website had the best buy?
_____

5 **READING** Read the advice on shopping in Tokyo. Then complete the statements and answer the questions on page 70.

TOKYO SHOPPING GUIDE
Below are descriptions of some of the best places to shop in Tokyo.

SOUVENIRS

"100-Yen" Shops
You can find 100-yen shops around many train stations and in some shopping areas. 100-yen shops are stores where most items cost 100 yen or less. In 100-yen shops, you can buy chopsticks, tableware, fans, kites, origami paper, calligraphy sets, "Hello Kitty" items, and much, much more! If you're looking for cheap souvenirs, 100-yen shops are the places to go.

Nakamise Shopping Arcade
This colorful, lively outdoor shopping street leads to the oldest temple in Tokyo. The walkway has been lined with souvenir shops and local food stands for centuries. You'll find paper umbrellas, kimonos, rice cakes, sweets, and much more. Prices are, for the most part, reasonable.

Oriental Bazaar
Oriental Bazaar is the largest and most famous souvenir shop in Tokyo. It has four floors, and the higher you go, the more expensive the items get. Here you can satisfy all of your gift-giving needs at reasonable prices.

ELECTRONICS

Akihabara
Looking for the latest electronic gadgets? Check out the Akihabara district. It's the place to find the newest cell phones, TVs, manga anime videos and computer games, and even miniature robot pets.

CLOTHING AND ACCESSORIES

Ginza
The Ginza is a famous high-end shopping district in Tokyo. It's full of upscale department stores and expensive designer boutiques. The fashions tend to be more conservative here. For younger and trendier styles, go to Shibuya or Harajuku.

1. _____ are the best places to find inexpensive souvenirs in Tokyo.
2. If you're interested in the latest technology, you might want to check out _____.
3. At _____, you might find a plastic samurai sword that's a steal in the basement and a traditional kimono that's a good deal on the top floor.
4. Prices are a bit steep here. If you're looking for a bargain, _____ is probably not the place to shop.
5. To pick up a few souvenirs, try some local snacks, and do a little sightseeing at the same time, _____ is a good bet.

_____

6. Where would you like to shop? Why? _____

LESSON 2

6 Think of something that happened to you or that you heard about recently that blew you away, got on your nerves, cracked you up, or choked you up. What was it? Why did it make you feel that way?

_____
_____

7 Complete each sentence with a passive gerund or infinitive. Use verbs from the box.

ask	entertain	ignore	treat
call	force	inform	

1. Alex can't stand _____ by telemarketers.
2. I enjoy _____ by funny commercials.
3. We hate _____ to watch ads before movies.
4. I appreciate _____ to join this company.
5. Scott hates _____.
6. Pam doesn't want _____ about new products.
7. My daughter dislikes _____ like a baby.

8 How do you feel about these forms of advertising? Write sentences with passive gerunds or infinitives. Use verbs from the box or your own verbs.

can't stand	don't appreciate	like	prefer
dislike	don't like	love	resent

1. Spam: _I don't appreciate being sent e-mail ads that I don't want._
2. Ads before movies: _____
3. Internet ads: _____
4. Direct mail: _____

5. Telemarketing calls: _____
6. Magazine ads: _____
7. Free product samples: _____
8. Product placement in movies: _____

LESSON 3

9 READING WARM-UP Answer the questions.

1. Do you enjoy shopping? _____
2. Do you feel comfortable shopping alone? _____
3. How often do you go shopping? _____
4. What do you buy for yourself? _____
5. Do you see a difference between men's and women's attitudes toward shopping?
   _____

10 READING Read about the shopping habits of North American men. Then answer the questions on page 72.

Shift in Men's Shopping Habits

According to recent studies, the shopping habits of men are changing significantly. In contrast to the traditional image of men as unwilling shoppers who aren't comfortable shopping for their own clothes, the new findings suggest that men now shop as a leisure activity, and that they make more impulse purchases of clothing than in the past.

Men are becoming independent and more confident shoppers. They're well-informed, willing to shop alone, and they are increasingly doing their clothing shopping online, comparing prices on retail websites, and making their own style decisions. Men are also paying more attention to fashion and are much more willing to experiment with style and splurge on fashion items than in the past.

In addition, the study found that men shop more often than in the past and are increasingly likely to buy certain products for themselves — especially electronics, casual clothing, watches, and fragrance or grooming products.

Unfortunately, shopping is almost as likely to become an addiction for men as it is for women. According to some estimates, about 6% of women and 5.5% of men are compulsive shoppers.

Among the findings of the studies:
- Men spend on average US $10 more per month on clothing than women do.
- Men prefer shopping on their phones: 45% of men shop for clothing on their phones, whereas 34% of women do.
- Women are much more likely to pay attention to sales than men are: 74% of women buy sale items online versus 54% of men.
- A luxury men's fashion shopping site says that its busiest days are Tuesdays and Fridays, when some famous luxury brands add new items to their website.
- The average age of male apparel shoppers is 30–39.

Now answer the questions.

1. According to the study, how are the shopping habits of men changing?
   _____
   _____

2. Do you think men's shopping habits are changing in a similar way in your country? Give examples to explain your answer.
   _____
   _____

3. Do you think the shift in men's shopping habits described in the article is a positive or a negative development? Explain your answer.
   _____
   _____

11 READING WARM-UP Answer the questions.

1. What country do you think does the most online shopping? _____
2. What do you think is the most popular online purchase? _____

12 READING Read about Internet shopping habits.

Trends in Online Shopping

According to recent surveys, more than 1.4 billion people have shopped online. Clothing and accessories were the most popular purchase, with over 50% of people indicating that they intended to purchase clothing online in the next six months. Purchases of clothing were followed closely by airline tickets and hotel reservations, event tickets, books (both hard copy and e-books), and personal care products.

Among the 30,000 people in 60 countries who were surveyed, people in Asia were the world's most frequent online shoppers, with 41–59% of respondents making online purchases. Asian shoppers were followed by those in Europe and the Middle East / Africa, while U.S. and Latin American shoppers made the fewest online purchases.

Online shoppers can also be broken down by age. The age group making the most online purchases worldwide is people ages 21–34, with 52–63% making purchases online. Following them are people ages 35–49, with 25–30% making online purchases. Most online shoppers preferred to use computers, though cell phone purchases are becoming increasingly popular worldwide, especially in Asia.

Why do global consumers shop online? One of the main attractions of Internet shopping is its convenience. Another feature of online shopping that is important to people is the ability to compare prices across many online retail sites. A final compelling reason given by a high percentage of respondents is simply that online shopping is fun.

In countries with widespread Internet access, some reasons people give for *not* shopping online include the expense of surfing, nervousness about using credit cards online, worries about companies collecting information about their shopping tastes, and reluctance to purchase goods from retailers they don't know.

Now answer the questions.

1. Were you surprised by the most popular online purchase? _____

2. Why do you think people buy more clothing than any other product online? _____

3. Why do you think more people use computers rather than cell phones for online shopping? Do you think this will change in the future? _____

4. Do any of the concerns about online shopping worry you? Why or why not? _____

13 Complete the chart by listing some advantages and disadvantages of shopping online.

Advantages	Disadvantages
It's easier to comparison shop.	

14 Check the items that you have purchased online.

- ☐ clothing / accessories / shoes
- ☐ hotel reservations or tour bookings
- ☐ music downloads
- ☐ books
- ☐ airline tickets
- ☐ event tickets
- ☐ electronic devices
- ☐ personal care products

Now circle the items you've purchased in the last month. How many online purchases do you think you've made in the last month? _____

15 Answer the questions.

1. Describe consumer shopping habits in your country—including online shopping. Do you see differences between older and younger shoppers? Between women and men?
___
___
___

2. Describe your own shopping habits. Are you a compulsive shopper? Do you ever indulge yourself? How often? Do you ever make impulse buys, or do you wait and shop when there is a sale?
___
___
___

LESSON 4

In 1991, the Swedish government banned advertising directed at children under the age of twelve.

16 Complete each sentence with a word from the box.

| endorse | imply | promote | prove |

1. My kids are really going to want to get their hands on those sneakers now that their favorite baseball player has agreed to _____ them.

2. I would buy the more expensive brand of toothpaste if the company could _____ that it's more effective at fighting cavities.

3. I heard First Choice Pizza is giving away free slices tonight to _____ its chain of restaurants.

4. The ads _____ that their competitor's cars are unsafe.

17 Look again at the list of advertising techniques on Student's Book page 82. Can you think of ads that use these techniques? Complete the chart for as many of the techniques as you can.

Advertising technique	Product	How the technique is used
Example: Provide facts and figures	ZX-10 MP3 player	The manufacturer states how many songs it holds, how little it weighs, and how many hours it can play.
1. Provide facts and figures		
2. Convince people to "jump on the bandwagon"		
3. Play on people's hidden fears		

W74 UNIT 7

Advertising technique	Product	How the technique is used
4. Play on people's patriotism		
5. Provide "snob appeal"		
6. Associate positive qualities with a product		
7. Provide testimonials		
8. Manipulate people's emotions		

Which of these techniques do you think is most effective? Why? _____

_____

GRAMMAR BOOSTER

A Rewrite each sentence in the passive voice.

1. Retailers all over the world sell our products.
   _____

2. Scott Joplin wrote that song.
   _____

3. Online stores are selling those shoes at a steep discount.
   _____

4. Jason Farah is going to endorse the new line of running shoes.
   _____

5. By the time we get to the concert hall, people will have taken all the good seats.
   _____

6. An ad that provides facts and figures can persuade Stu.
   _____

7. CompTech has hired Ella to design its website.
   _____

8. City Symphony is going to perform a new opera tonight.
   _____

B Rewrite each of your sentences from Exercise A as a yes / no question.

1. _____
2. _____
3. _____
4. _____
5. _____
6. _____
7. _____
8. _____

C Complete each question in the passive voice.

1. **A:** When _____?
   B: Our house was built in 1920.

2. **A:** What time _____?
   B: Lunch will be served at 12:30.

3. **A:** How long _____?
   B: We were given 2 hours to complete the test.

4. **A:** Where _____?
   B: The party will be held at City Hall.

5. **A:** _____?
   B: No, she's not being given an award tonight.

6. **A:** _____ yet?
   B: No, the house hasn't been sold yet.

WRITING: Summarize and paraphrase someone's point of view

Choose one of the following articles to summarize:

- *Bird-poop Facials*, Workbook page 39–40
- *Questionable Cosmetic Treatments*, Student's Book page 44
- *The Will to Make a Difference*, Student's Book page 70
- An article you've read outside of class

A PREWRITING: IDENTIFYING MAIN IDEAS Read the article you've chosen and underline or highlight the important parts. Then read the article again and list the main ideas below. (The article you have chosen may have fewer than six paragraphs.)

| Main idea of paragraph 1: |
| Main idea of paragraph 2: |
| Main idea of paragraph 3: |
| Main idea of paragraph 4: |
| Main idea of paragraph 5: |
| Main idea of paragraph 6: |

B WRITING Combine the main ideas to write your summary. Be sure to paraphrase what the author says, using your own words. Your summary should have one or two sentences for every paragraph in the original article.

Reporting verbs:
argue   point out
believe   report
conclude   state
explain

Common expressions:
According to _____,
In _____'s opinion,
As _____ explains,
From _____'s point of view,

C SELF-CHECK

☐ Does the summary include only the author's main ideas?
☐ Did I paraphrase the author's ideas?
☐ Was I careful not to include my opinion in the summary?

UNIT 8

Family Trends

PREVIEW

1 Read each situation. Then complete each sentence summarizing what happened. Use the expressions from the box and your own words. One of the situations will use two expressions.

behind her back	~~have a falling out~~	split up
fall apart	hit the nail on the head	
going downhill	patch things up	

1. Tina and her sister Marie had a big fight last month. They weren't speaking to each other for a few weeks. But I just heard that they got together and talked and worked everything out. Now they're just as close as they were before. I'm so glad.

    Tina and Marie _____had a falling out_____, but then _____.

2. Sara is coming to the party, but Gary isn't. I heard that they're not together any more. It's really too bad.

    Sara and Gary _____.

3. Did you hear that Jason just quit his job? He got a new boss earlier this year, and I guess things at the office just started getting worse and worse. Finally, Jason had enough and couldn't take anymore.

    _____, and finally Jason quit his job.

4. I was wondering why they hadn't arrived yet, but I think you're exactly right, Tom — they must be stuck in traffic.

    Tom _____.

5. Jan and Mike were going to buy an apartment in the city. But at the last minute, the people who were selling the apartment decided not to sell.

    Jan and Mike were going to buy an apartment, but then _____.

6. Marsha told me that she doesn't like Peggy. It made me uncomfortable to hear that she thought Peggy was selfish.

    Marsha _____.

2 How can parents raise well-behaved kids who won't turn into troublemakers? Write sentences using <u>should</u> or <u>shouldn't</u>.

Should	Shouldn't
Kids should be given clear rules to follow.	Kids shouldn't be criticized constantly.

LESSON 1

3 Rewrite each sentence with a repeated comparative so that the sentence describes a trend. (Some sentences can be rewritten more than one way.)

1. People are moving to cities to find work.
   More and more people are moving to cities to find work.
2. People are spending long hours at work.
   People are spending longer and longer hours at work.
3. Men are getting involved in caring for their children.
   _____
4. People are spending time with their extended families.
   _____
5. Mothers are staying home to take care of their children.
   _____
6. Couples are choosing to remain childless.
   _____
7. Young adults are moving out of their parents' homes.
   _____
8. Adolescents receive adult supervision.
   _____

4 Complete the sentences, using double comparatives. Use the correct form of each word from the box.

develop	few	good	less	low	more

1. _____ people work, _____ time they spend with their families.
2. _____ a country is, _____ the healthcare system.
3. _____ the birthrate, _____ children there will be to care for older members of society.

few	good	high	long	more	old

4. _____ education you have, _____ your salary will be.
5. _____ the health-care system, _____ people live.
6. _____ people are when they get married, _____ children they are likely to have.

> According to a study by the United Nations, by the middle of the 21st century the birth rate in 139 countries will not be high enough to replace the existing population.

Family Trends   W79

5 Complete each double comparative. Use your own ideas.

1. The longer I live, _____.
2. The harder you work, _____.
3. The more that you read, _____.
4. The better I get to know people, _____.
5. The more things change, _____.

Now compare your sentences with these famous quotes.

> "The longer I live, the more beautiful life becomes."
> —Frank Lloyd Wright, architect (1869–1959)

> "The harder you work, the luckier you get."
> —Samuel Goldwyn, movie producer (1882–1974)

> "The more that you read, the more things you will know. The more that you learn, the more places you'll go."
> —Dr. Seuss, children's book author (1904–1991)

> "The better I get to know men, the more I find myself loving dogs."
> —Charles De Gaulle, French leader (1890–1970)

> "The more things change, the more they are the same."
> —Alphonse Karr, author (1808–1890)

Choose one of the quotes and describe what it means. How does it apply to your life and/or to the world today?

_____
_____
_____

LESSON 2

6 What do you think parents should do if their teenaged kids start smoking? Read each idea and decide how effective you think it would be.

Parents should . . .	ineffective	somewhat effective	very effective
accept that there's not much they can do.	○	○	○
talk to their kids about the health risks of smoking.	○	○	○
ask their kids questions to find out why they are smoking.	○	○	○
ground them.	○	○	○
let their kids know that they disapprove of their smoking.	○	○	○
talk to their kids about other negative effects of smoking, such as poor sports performance, smelly clothes and hair, bad breath, and yellow teeth.	○	○	○
allow their kids to make their own mistakes.	○	○	○
explain how the tobacco industry's advertising targets young people to become smokers.	○	○	○

(continued)

Parents should...	ineffective	somewhat effective	very effective
have their kids visit people who have lung cancer.	○	○	○
not make a big deal about a little bit of rebellious behavior.	○	○	○
quit smoking themselves if they are smokers.	○	○	○

What do you think is the best idea? Why? _____

_____

7 Read the teen blog entries and describe the teens' or their parents' behavior. Use the vocabulary from Student's Book page 90.

💬 Comment   ➔ Share

1. Posted: 10:09 AM

Princess5574
Hey! It's my birthday! When I woke up this morning, I went downstairs and opened the gifts my parents had left for me. I got some jewelry, some clothes, a new laptop — nothing special. I was a little disappointed. But when I walked out of the house, I found my real present in the driveway! My sports car — exactly the one I had asked for. I can't wait to drive it to my party on Saturday. REPLY

2. Posted: 11:48 AM

Nolife312
They gave you a car? My parents won't even let me learn how to drive, or go anywhere in anyone else's car – or ride my bike down the street! They're afraid I'll hurt myself, I guess. I need to be able to hang out with my friends, go to the movies, maybe even go to a party every once in a while. I love my parents, but they're ruining my life! REPLY

3. Posted: 1:02 PM

Norules721
Well, at least your parents care about what you do. My parents let me go where I want, do what I want. They don't mind if I invite the whole school over for a party. I know they love me, but I wish they would stop trying to be "cool" and act more like parents. REPLY

4. Posted: 1:34 PM

Noworries219
My parents set rules about everything. From the moment I get up, they watch every move I make and put restrictions on everything. But I don't care. I do what I want. If I want to go to a party, and they say I can't, I just sneak out and go anyway! REPLY

1. _Princess is spoiled. Her parents are_ _____
2. _____
3. _____
4. _____

8 **WHAT ABOUT YOU?** Check the sentences that describe your upbringing.

Lenient upbringing	Strict upbringing
○ My parents did things for me that I could or should have done for myself.	○ My parents made me do many things for myself.
○ My parents did not expect me to do many chores or to help much around the house.	○ I had to do a lot of chores around the house.
○ I was allowed to have almost any clothes I wanted.	○ I had to use my own money to buy clothes.
○ My parents gave me too much freedom.	○ I wasn't given very much freedom.
○ My parents allowed me to take the lead or dominate the family.	○ My parents used physical punishment to discipline me.
○ My parents did not enforce their rules.	○ My parents set a lot of rules for me to follow.

Do you think you were spoiled as a child? Were your parents too strict? Or did you grow up with a nice balance between strictness and leniency? Explain and try to give examples.

_____
_____
_____

What should parents do (or not do) to raise kids who aren't spoiled? List some ideas.

_____
_____
_____

LESSON 3

9 Match the words with their definitions. Write the letter on the line.

1. _____ frustration
2. _____ involvement
3. _____ courtesy
4. _____ maturity
5. _____ obedience

a. willingness to do what someone in a position of authority tells you to do

b. the quality of behaving in a sensible way and like an adult

c. the act of taking part in an activity or event, or the way in which you take part in it

d. the feeling of being annoyed, upset, or impatient because you cannot control or change a situation or achieve something

e. polite behavior that shows that you have respect for other people

10 CHALLENGE Choose the best word to complete each sentence.

1. His parents intend for him to get married as soon as he finishes college. That is their ____.
   a. explanation   b. importance   c. expectation   d. impatience

2. Carl Brooks is almost thirty-eight years old and still living in his parents' home. His parents resent his ____.
   a. dependence   b. dependability   c. development   d. difference

3. Her parents don't think she should change jobs again. They worry about her long-term financial ____.
   a. mobility   b. security   c. lenience   d. confidence

4. Dana Wolf doesn't like her daughter's new boyfriend. She thinks he's lazy and disrespectful. She can't understand her daughter's ____ to him.
   a. attractiveness   b. consideration   c. involvement   d. attraction

5. The company's ____ improved after they hired three new employees.
   a. productive   b. maturity   c. productivity   d. responsibility

11 Answer the questions.

1. What is a "generation gap"?
   _____

2. What developments (political, technological, social, etc.) do you think have contributed to the generation gap between your generation and that of your parents?
   _____
   _____

3. In what ways are your generation and that of your parents similar?
   _____
   _____

LESSON 4

12 READING WARM-UP How are the responsibilities of caring for children different from those of caring for the elderly? How are they the same?
_____
_____
_____
_____

13 READING Read the article.

The Sandwich Generation

In the United States and Canada they've been termed the sandwich generation—people caught between the needs of their growing children and their aging parents, having to care for both. Factors giving rise to the sandwich generation include the fact that people are having children later in life, combined with longer life expectancies. Whatever the cause, this new responsibility places many demands on these caregivers' time and energy and leaves little space for attending to their own needs.

Some members of the sandwich generation are parents in their 30s or 40s caring for young children. For example, Pamela Bose, 40, has a three-year-old and a nine-year-old. She has recently taken over the care of her widowed mother. One minute she is worrying about getting the children to school on time; the next, she is checking to make sure that her mother has remembered to take her medicine. "I spend so much time keeping up with their competing demands that I end up not devoting enough time to anyone, let alone making time for myself," says Bose.

Other members of the sandwich generation are parents in their 40s or 50s caring for teenaged or adult children. Nowadays, more adult children are living at home while they're in college and even afterward, as they get established and figure out what they want to do. Also, an increasing number of adult children are returning home to live after a divorce or job loss.

The longer adult children remain dependent on their parents, the more people find themselves in the sandwich generation. Patricia Rivas is one of these people. She and her husband David both have careers. They have a teenaged son, a recently divorced daughter with a two-year-old child, and an elderly father who has early dementia and is requiring more and more care, all living in the same household.

Most sandwich-generation caregivers are women. Increased female labor-force participation means that many of these women are balancing not only care for their children and parents but also their own careers. Without a doubt, trying to meet all of these obligations at the same time is stressful. It's not surprising that sandwich-generation members report an increase in depression, sleeplessness, headaches, and other health problems. While many are happy about the chance to help care for their parents, they also feel guilty about not doing more.

As sandwich-generation members try to respond to everyone else's needs, it's important that they not ignore their own needs. As these caregivers struggle to give their young children attention and patience, their older children support and guidance, their elderly parents physical care and opportunities for social interaction and inclusion in family life, it is also important that they make some time for their own relaxation. Unfortunately, such relaxation is more often than not overlooked.

Now answer the questions.

1. What is the "sandwich generation"?

   _____

2. How is the term "sandwich" appropriate to describe this generation?

   _____

3. Name three trends that are responsible for the development of the "sandwich generation."
   _____
   _____
   _____

4. What are some problems that sandwich-generation members experience?
   _____
   _____

5. Why is being a member of the sandwich generation especially stressful for women?
   _____
   _____

14 Look back at the article in Exercise 13. Find the nouns that correspond to the verbs and adjectives below. Write them on the lines.

1. responsible: _____
2. participate: _____
3. obligate: _____
4. depress: _____
5. sleepless: _____
6. patient: _____
7. guide: _____
8. interact: _____
9. include: _____
10. relax: _____

Life expectancy in the People's Republic of China was around 40 years in the middle of the 20th century. By 2010, it had risen to around 75 years.

In the U.S., approximately 47 percent of people between the ages of 45 and 55 have children under 21 and also have aging parents or in-laws.

15 Do you know anyone who is caring for his or her children and/or an elderly family member? Describe the person's situation. What challenges is he or she facing?

Family Trends   W85

GRAMMAR BOOSTER

A Read each pair of statements. Then complete each sentence, using a comparative, superlative, or comparison with <u>as</u> . . . <u>as</u>.

1. Today's hike is 5 km. But our hike yesterday was 7 km.

    Today's hike is *shorter than yesterday's hike*.

2. A cheetah can run 96 km per hour. A greyhound can run 64 km per hour.

    A greyhound can't run _____.

3. I am 24 years old. My brother is 20, and my sister is 18.

    Of the three of us, I am _____.

4. Park City is 5 km from here. Greenville is 10 km from here.

    Greenville is _____.

5. His parents are very strict. My parents are not very strict.

    My parents are _____.

6. Mr. Plant has two children. Mr. Lane has four children.

    Mr. Plant has _____.

7. I paint well. Ten years ago, I didn't paint well.

    I paint _____.

8. There are five people in my family. There are five people in Irene Lee's family, too.

    There are _____.

9. My commute to work is 14 km. My colleague Mrs. Young has a 20 km commute, and my other colleague, Mr. Davis, travels 30 km to work.

    Of the three of us, I have _____.

10. My grandmother is 80 years old. My grandfather is 78 years old.

    My grandfather isn't _____.

11. When Nina was younger, she needed ten hours of sleep each night. Now she is a teenager, and she needs only eight hours of sleep each night.

    Now that Nina is a teenager, she needs _____.

B Compare people and things you know. Use comparatives or <u>as</u> . . . <u>as</u>.

Example: two friends — adventurous

<u>Megan is more adventurous than Matthew.</u>

1. two friends — adventurous

2. two movies — funny

3. two books — long

4. two stores — expensive

5. two TV shows — good

6. two singers — sing well

7. two family members — work hard

C Complete each statement. Use your own idea in the first blank and a superlative in the second.

1. <u>Liver</u> is <u>the worst</u> thing I've ever eaten.
2. _____ is _____ person I've ever met.
3. _____ is _____ place I've ever been.
4. _____ is _____ thing I've ever done.
5. _____ is _____ thing I've ever bought.
6. _____ is _____ thing I've ever said.

D **CHALLENGE** Read each sentence. Then write a sentence with similar meaning, using a comparative, a superlative, or <u>as</u> . . . <u>as</u>.

1. At 421 meters, the Jin Mao Building in Shanghai is very tall.

   <u>The Jin Mao Building in Shanghai is more than 400 meters tall.</u>

2. The population of Greenland is only 56,238.

3. The movie we watched last night was so depressing.

4. Alexis McCarthy is becoming a very good violin player because she practices daily.

5. Sometimes he watches TV, but usually he reads.

6. The new French restaurant on City Avenue looks expensive, but it's really not.

Family Trends

WRITING: Avoiding run-on sentences and comma splices

A **PREWRITING: COMPARE & CONTRAST CHART** Choose a family member of a different generation from you. Write his or her name in the box next to "ME." Then fill in the chart with how your generations are similar and how they are different.

COMPARING GENERATIONS

| ME | _____ |

Similarities

Differences

B **WRITING** Write one or two paragraphs comparing the two generations you chose. Include a topic sentence that expresses your main idea. Avoid run-on sentences and comma splices.

C **SELF-CHECK**

☐ Did I avoid run-on sentences and comma splices?
☐ Do all the sentences support the topic sentence?
☐ Did I use the vocabulary and expressions I learned in this unit?

UNIT 9
Facts, Theories, and Hoaxes

PREVIEW

1 Read the stories below. Rate the probability that each is true.

1. A couple was on vacation in Australia, driving through the bush, when they accidentally hit a kangaroo. They decided to prop the kangaroo up and take a photo. To add a bit of humor, they dressed it up in the husband's jacket.
   As it turned out, the kangaroo was only stunned, not dead, and it hopped away with the jacket on. In the jacket pocket were the keys to their rental car and all their vacation money.

2. A college student stayed up late studying for a math final exam. He overslept and arrived late for the test. He found three problems written on the board. He solved the first two pretty easily but struggled with the third. He worked frantically and figured out a solution just before the time was up.
   That night the student received a phone call from his professor, who told him that the third problem wasn't a test question. Before the test had started, the professor had explained that it was a problem previously thought to be unsolvable. But the student had solved it!

3. A man was jogging through the park one day when another jogger lightly bumped him and excused himself. The man was just a little annoyed—until he realized that his wallet was missing. He immediately began chasing the jogger who'd bumped into him. He caught up to him and tackled him, yelling, "Give me that wallet!" The frightened "thief" handed over a wallet and quickly ran off.
   When the man got home, his wife asked him if he'd remembered to stop at the store. Anxious to tell his story, the man said that he hadn't, but that he had a good excuse. Before he finished, his wife said, "I know—you left your wallet on the dresser."

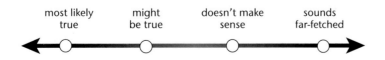

W89

2 Now put the conversation about the third story on the previous page in order. Write numbers on the lines.

_____ What? You've heard it before?

_____ What happened?

_____ It's a story that people pass on, about something unusual that happened to an ordinary person. A lot of people believe them, but they're usually not true.

_1_ You'll never guess what happened to a friend of a friend's husband.

_____ Yeah, I have. The jogger took the other guy's wallet and then got home and realized he had left his wallet at home. It's an urban legend.

_____ Wow. I had no idea. It seemed believable.

_____ Well, he was jogging in the park, and this guy bumped into him. He thought the guy had stolen his wallet, so he chased him and tackled him . . .

_____ What's an urban legend?

_____ Don't tell me you buy that story!

3 **CHALLENGE** Do you know any urban legends or fantastic stories? Write one of them in your own words.

_____
_____
_____
_____
_____
_____

4 Complete the conversation with phrases from the box.

| going out on a limb | doesn't make sense |
| barking up the wrong tree | vanished without a trace |

A: My wallet is missing. It was in my purse, but it seems to have _____. Someone at the party must have taken it.

B: Hmm. I think you're _____.

A: What do you mean?

B: It _____. You know almost everyone who was at the party. I may be _____ here, but I think you probably just misplaced it.

A: You're probably right.

LESSON 1

5 Complete the conversations. Speculate about the situations, using vocabulary from Student's Book page 100.

1. **A:** My dad was supposed to meet me after school at 3:30. It's 4:05, and he's still not here.
   B: _____

2. **A:** Lisa was supposed to call me half an hour ago. I wonder why she hasn't called.
   B: _____

3. **A:** My dog usually loves going for walks, but today she won't even come outside with me. What do you think could be wrong?
   B: _____

4. **A:** Usually the sanitation department picks up the trash on Monday mornings. It's 4 P.M., and they still haven't picked up the trash on my street.
   B: _____

5. **A:** I bought tickets to see the Velvet Overboards in concert this weekend. I was really excited, but I just heard that they cancelled the concert. I have no idea why.
   B: _____

6. **A:** The new employee was supposed to start today, but he hasn't come to work. I wonder what happened?
   B: _____

6 Read the situation below. Then, for each of the times listed, write a sentence about what could have happened. Use vocabulary from Student's Book page 100.

Example: (8:10) Not certain: _Maybe she's getting her luggage._

1. (8:10) Not certain: _____
2. (8:20) Almost certain: _____
3. (8:35) Very certain: _____

Your friend was supposed to arrive on the 8:05 train. You are waiting outside the station, but she still isn't there.

7 Rewrite the sentences with perfect modals in the active voice.

1. Clearly, the ancient Greeks didn't build an underwater city.
   <u>The ancient Greeks couldn't have built an underwater city.</u>

2. Most likely people used the statues for religious ceremonies.
   _____

3. The Egyptians who built the pyramids probably used sleds to move large blocks of stone.
   _____

4. Those patterns in the earth were definitely not made by aliens.
   _____

5. It's possible that a storm caused all this damage.
   _____

6. Clearly, this was an important place for the early inhabitants.
   _____

8 Read each statement and check whether each speaker is <u>very certain</u>, <u>almost certain</u>, or <u>not certain</u>. Then rewrite each sentence, using a perfect modal in the passive voice. Use the appropriate degree of certainty.

very certain	almost certain	not certain	
☐	☐	☑	1. It's possible that language was initially developed to allow humans to hunt in groups more effectively. <u>Language may have been developed to allow humans to hunt in groups more effectively.</u>
☐	☐	☐	2. Maybe the dinosaurs were killed by climate changes.
☐	☐	☐	3. Probably the giant stone statues on Easter Island were carved by the ancestors of the Polynesian people who live there today.
☐	☐	☐	4. Most likely Amelia Earhart was killed when her plane ran out of fuel and went down in the Pacific Ocean.
☐	☐	☐	5. Clearly, the fire was started intentionally.
☐	☐	☐	6. There's no question the ship was sunk by a collision with an iceberg.

9 **READING WARM-UP** Look at the picture and caption. Then speculate about what happened to the *Mary Celeste,* using the perfect form of the modal <u>may</u> in the passive voice.

Example: *The crew may have been washed overboard by a giant wave.*

Your speculation: _____

_____

The *Mary Celeste* was discovered drifting off the coast of Portugal in 1872. There was no one aboard.

10 **READING** Read more about the circumstances surrounding the disappearance of the *Mary Celeste's* crew and passengers.

The Mary Celeste

On November 7, 1872, the *Mary Celeste* sailed under the command of Captain Benjamin Briggs—known as an honest and fair man. He, his wife, young daughter, and a crew of seven departed from New York City for Genoa, Italy, carrying a cargo of alcohol. They were never seen again.

On December 4, another ship spotted the *Mary Celeste* drifting off the coast of Portugal. A few men from the ship boarded the *Mary Celeste* to offer help. Although there was some damage, it was not extensive, and the ship was seaworthy. The cargo and a six-month supply of food and water were still on board the ship. However, nine of the 1,700 barrels of alcohol were empty, and the lifeboat and all of the passengers and crew were missing. The last entry in the logbook was dated November 24, 1872.

Many theories have been proposed to explain the mystery of the disappearance of the *Mary Celeste's* crew and passengers. Here are some of them:

• The crew killed Captain Briggs and his family and escaped in the lifeboat.

• The nine barrels of alcohol had leaked. Afraid the fumes would cause an explosion, Captain Briggs ordered everyone into the lifeboat. The lifeboat got separated from the ship, and its occupants drowned or died at sea.

• A giant octopus snatched the crew one by one from the deck of the ship.

Now speculate about the probability of each theory explaining the disappearance of the *Mary Celeste's* passengers and crew. Use perfect modals in the passive voice. Explain your answers.

1. The theory that the captain was killed by the crew:

_____

_____

2. The theory that the crew was forced by alcohol fumes to leave the ship:

_____

_____

3. The theory that the crew was snatched from the ship by a giant octopus:

_____

_____

LESSON 3

11 Complete the paragraph, using <u>believable</u>, <u>debatable</u>, <u>unprovable</u>, or <u>questionable</u>.

I recently received an e-mail message of _____ truthfulness. Of course,
                                              1.
whether or not it's a good idea to even open these types of forwarded messages is

_____. However, I did open it. According to the e-mail story, a woman and
      2.

her daughter had enjoyed a delicious cookie in the café of a high-end department store in the United

States. The cookie was so good that the woman asked for the recipe. The server replied that woman

could purchase the recipe for "two fifty." The woman agreed and asked that the charge be added to

her credit card bill. When the woman received her bill in the mail, the charge for the cookie recipe was

two hundred and fifty dollars—not two dollars and fifty cents. I guess a lot of people must find this

story _____, because the message keeps getting forwarded. Personally, I don't buy the
           3.

story. Of course, the story is not completely _____. All you would have to do is go to
                                                     4.

the store's café and ask to buy the cookie recipe—and pay in cash.

12 **READING WARM-UP** Have you ever heard a story you thought was questionable or a hoax? Write the story below. How believable is it? Is it provable?

_____

_____

_____

_____

13 **READING** Read the article.

On the evening of Sunday, October 30, 1938, people listening to their radios in the U.S. received some terrifying news: CBS radio was reporting that explosions had been detected on the planet Mars, and that alien spaceships had landed in New Jersey. The radio announcer reported "live" from the landing site, describing the fearsome creatures that emerged from the ships. Next, the radio reported that the Martians were apparently advancing on New York City, killing anything that came in their path. Soon after, the radio reported that Martian ships had also landed in Chicago, Illinois, and St. Louis, Missouri.

In 1938, radio was a major source of news and entertainment, with people listening to programs for information, just as people often get information from their TV's or computers today. Estimates are that possibly a million people heard the broadcast and panicked, sure that the Earth was under Martian attack. Highways became jammed with traffic as terrified people attempted to escape the areas in which the ships had landed.

In reality, the "reports" were all part of a radio adaptation of a science fiction novel by H.G. Wells titled *War of the Worlds*. The program was performed live on the radio by the Mercury Theater company, headed by actor and director Orson Welles. (Though the names are similar, the author and actor were not related.)

At the beginning of the radio broadcast, Welles announced that the program was a performance of the story, but many people had turned on their radios after the program had already started and missed that announcement. Welles and the other actors used state-of-the-art equipment for sound effects and worked hard to make their program sound like a real radio news broadcast. They succeeded beyond what anyone had expected. Welles was even forced to go back on the air to reassure people that what they had heard was actually fiction.

Welles said later that no one had ever intended to fool the public. In fact, according to some of the actors involved, many people thought that listeners would be bored by the performance or would think it was ridiculous. They couldn't have known that people would think the broadcast was real. Welles himself was afraid that it would be a complete failure. Instead, *War of the Worlds* launched his career, and he went on to be a much-celebrated movie director and actor.

Now answer the questions.

1. What was *War of the Worlds*?

2. What was its effect on people in the U.S.?

3. Do you find it believable that Welles didn't intend to fool people?

4. Imagine you had heard the program. Do you think you could have been fooled? Why or why not?

5. What do you think you would have done if you had believed the broadcast?

14 Look back at the article in Exercise 13. Answer the questions.

1. Do you think CBS radio was to blame for the panic that *War of the Worlds* caused? Explain.

2. What, if anything, do you think the broadcasting company should have done differently?

3. In 1938, people didn't have the Internet to fact-check what they heard on the radio. How else do you think they could have determined if the "news" they were hearing was true?

15 Describe a story that you didn't believe at first, but which turned out to be true, or one that you initially believed, but which turned out to be false. Where did you first hear the story? How did you find out the truth?

_____
_____
_____
_____
_____
_____

GRAMMAR BOOSTER

A Match the questions and answers. Write the letter on the line.

_____ 1. Did the early inhabitants here grow their own food?

_____ 2. Do you think the Nazca Lines were carved by aliens?

_____ 3. Did I write that letter? I can't remember.

_____ 4. I wonder if the photo of the sea monster was created on a computer.

_____ 5. Do you think the package came from Jennifer?

_____ 6. Do you think Steven was fooled by the story?

a. They couldn't have been.
b. It might have.
c. They must have.
d. It must have been.
e. He might have been.
f. You must have.

B Respond to each statement or question with a short response, using the perfect modal in parentheses.

1. **A:** I wonder if there really was a person named King Arthur.
   B: _____ (could)

2. **A:** Do you think people used water to move the stones?
   B: _____ (might)

3. **A:** Was the newspaper story of aliens in London a hoax?
   B: _____ (had to)

4. **A:** Were the monkeys moved to a different area of the zoo last night?
   B: _____ (must)

5. **A:** Do you think the crew of the *Mary Celeste* was snatched by a giant octopus?
   B: _____ (couldn't)

6. **A:** Do you think Falcon Heene's father knew how upset Falcon would be?
   B: _____ (might)

WRITING: Avoiding sentence fragments

A **PREWRITING: MIND MAP** Think about the time you made a new friend. Recall details of the meeting using the questions on the mind map. Expand each branch as necessary. Use words or sentences. Don't worry about grammar or punctuation.

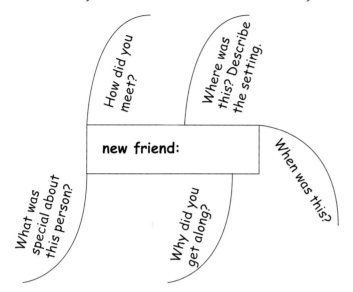

WRITING MODEL

A New Friend

Last summer I made a new friend while on vacation in Italy. I was hiking in a region called Cinque Terre when I met a man named Flavio. We discovered that we both spoke English, and we began talking. We got along so well that he invited me back to his family's home for lunch. I met his mother, father, and brothers and sisters. His mother made a delicious lunch, and we ate it in their beautiful home overlooking the ocean. I spent a delightful afternoon with Flavio and his family, and by the end of the day we were friends. We still write to each other, and I plan to visit again next year.

B **WRITING** Use the mind map to write about meeting a new friend. Try to include as many interesting details as possible. Choose a title that reflects your main idea. Make sure to avoid sentence fragments.

_____
_____
_____
_____
_____
_____
_____
_____
_____
_____
_____
_____

C **SELF-CHECK**

☐ Do all my sentences express complete thoughts?

☐ Did I avoid sentence fragments?

☐ Did I avoid run-on sentences?

UNIT 10

Your Free Time

PREVIEW

1 Answer the questions.

1. Where do you like to hang out with your friends? _____
2. Where do you go to relax? _____
3. What's your idea of excitement? _____
4. What TV shows do you watch? _____
5. What sports do you play? _____
6. Do you attend sports events? Which ones? _____
7. Do you attend cultural events? What have you been to lately? _____
   _____
8. What are your hobbies? _____

2 **WHAT ABOUT YOU?** Complete the survey.

About how much time do you spend on the Internet each day? _____

What do you do on the Internet? Check all the activities you engage in.

- ○ e-mail
- ○ news
- ○ games
- ○ shopping
- ○ banking
- ○ music
- ○ chat/instant messaging
- ○ information searches
- ○ surfing
- ○ other: _____

Do you think you spend too much time online?
_____

If you didn't have Internet access, what would you spend more time doing?
_____
_____

3 Write the name of a person you know for each category. Provide examples.

1. Someone who's sociable: _____
2. A loner: _____
3. Someone who's active: _____
4. Someone who's sedentary: _____
5. Someone who's laid back: _____

4 Answer the questions.

1. Do you ever feel like you're on call for work or something else? Explain. _____
   _____

2. Do you have a lot on your plate right now? Give examples. _____
   _____

3. Have you ever slacked off on a project or obligation? What happened? _____
   _____

4. Describe a time when you were a nervous wreck. _____
   _____

5. Describe a time when you gave it your all. Was it worth it? _____
   _____

> **Tips for maintaining work-life balance**
> 1. Don't do work on your commute home. Use the time to unwind.
> 2. At the end of every work day, write a list of unfinished tasks and when you will complete them. Then stop thinking about them.
> 3. Exercise after work. It's a great way to reduce stress.
> 4. Don't check work e-mail once you get home.
> 5. Schedule time to do nothing. It's okay to just relax!

LESSON 1

5 Give each person some advice. Use phrases from the box.

| learn to laugh things off | set limits | take a breather |
| set aside some down time | slow down | take up a hobby |

I've been working on this report all day without a break. I'm getting a headache.

I've been working so much lately — weekends, too. And when I'm not working, I'm attending class or studying!

1. You really should take a breather now and then.

2. _____

Let's see... I have to finish this report by 12, then I have a quick lunch meeting, then I have to run across town for another meeting, and from there I hope to catch the 5:30 train.

My colleagues have started calling me at home to discuss work. I'm not sure what to do about it.

3. _____

4. _____

Did you hear what Kevin said? He made fun of my tie!

I don't feel like I'm very interesting. All I do is work. Work and eat and sleep.

5. _____

6. _____

6 Choose the correct word or phrase to complete each sentence.

1. Ella _____ have a piano lesson tomorrow.
   a. is supposed to
   b. will be supposed to

2. He _____ park there.
   a. didn't suppose to
   b. wasn't supposed to

3. _____ turn in our homework yesterday?
   a. Weren't we supposed to   b. Aren't we supposed to
4. Where _____ meet the tour group?
   a. we're supposed to   b. are we supposed to
5. Is this movie _____ good?
   a. supposed to be   b. supposed

7 Complete the sentences expressing expectations with <u>be supposed to</u>.
1. (We / arrive at 5:00) <u>We're supposed to arrive at 5:00</u> tomorrow.
2. (They / not / open their gifts) _____ before we get there.
3. (When / Tina / take a break) _____ and rest? She looks tired.
4. (We / go hiking) _____ yesterday, but it rained.
5. (Who / wash the dishes) _____ last night?
6. (Loretta and Bob / come) _____ to the party later.
7. (Peter / visit) _____ this afternoon? I'll make sure I'm here.
8. (You / not smoke) _____ in here. Would you mind going outside?

LESSON 2

8 Correct the errors in these sentences.
1. When I was young, I was ride my bike wherever I went.
2. Mario would always building something when he was a kid.
3. We would love being outside all summer long when we were younger.
4. My brother used to helping our neighbors shovel snow.
5. In her childhood, Nadia was always play in the snow with her sister.

9 CHALLENGE Circle the correct words or phrases to complete the paragraph.

My sister and I had a wonderful childhood. We grew up in the country, and we made the most of it. There was a special place in the woods where we (1. would play / were always playing) every day. Lots of wildflowers grew there, and we (2. was always picking / would pick) lots of them to take home. It seemed like we (3. were always doing / used to do) something outside. We had a dog, and she (4. used to like / would like) to come with us wherever we went. She (5. used to be running / was always running) ahead of us, but as soon as we called her, she (6. would come / was always coming) right back to us. In the winter, we (7. would enjoy / used to enjoy) the outdoors just as much. We (8. would play / were always playing) in the snow for a while, but then we (9. would end up / were ending up) having a snowball fight. I have many happy memories of those times.

10 **WHAT ABOUT YOU?** What is a hobby you'd like to try? What do you think you would like about it? What do you need to do to get started?

___

LESSON 3

11 How do new technological tools make people's lives easier? How do they take away from leisure time? Name one positive aspect and one negative aspect of each of the technologies listed.

Technology	Positive	Negative
cell phones		
tablets		
laptops		
e-mail		
texting		

12 Read the article on Student's Book page 116 again. Then complete the sentence below in three different ways, using double comparatives.

According to the author, the more we use our devices...

___

13 Think about your day yesterday. Answer the questions.

1. How many hours did you spend working or studying? ___

2. How much free time did you have? What did you do? ___

3. If you work, did you work after hours? What technological tools did you use to do your work? ___

4. Did you talk to any friends yesterday? If so, did you see them in person, talk to them on the phone, or send them an e-mail or a text message? ___

14 READING Read the article.

... Work at Home, Play at Work ...

Thanks to the Internet and other relatively new technological tools, more and more employees work after hours. They check their e-mail before they go to bed at night, take business calls while out to dinner with friends, and check their text messages at family picnics. Nowadays, if you're sick, you don't have to take a day off. Why waste a day sleeping and watching movies when, with a laptop and an Internet connection, you can work from home? It seems that the line between work and leisure has become blurry and that more technology for work has meant less time for ourselves.

However, technology has not only helped work invade people's leisure time, but it has also allowed people to engage in leisure-time activities at work. With the computer on your office desk, you can leave work virtually. You can check the score of last night's game, do a little shopping, catch up on the news, order concert tickets, plan a vacation, chat with your friends, or just browse the Web. You can appear to be working hard—plugging away at your computer—when in reality you're reading a fashion magazine online.

According to a recent survey, more than half of the employees questioned said they spent between one and five hours a day surfing the Internet at work for personal reasons. There are even websites dedicated to keeping bored workers amused while they wait for the end of the work day. A psychotherapist who treats Internet addiction explains, "It's like having a TV at everyone's desk. People can watch whatever they want and do whatever they want."

Perhaps a more definite separation of work and home life would be better not only for employees but also for employers. It's not healthy for workers to have access to work 24/7*. And maybe if employees weren't busy working at night and on the weekends, they wouldn't have to e-mail their friends while they're at work.

* 24/7 = 24 hours a day, 7 days a week

Now complete each sentence with a word or phrase from the article.

1. If something is not clear, it's _____.
2. When something unwanted interferes with your time, it _____ your time.
3. If you do something on a computer, rather than in the real world, you do it _____.
4. If you're working hard at something, you're _____ at it.
5. If you do something all the time, you do it _____.

15 Answer the questions, using information from the article in Exercise 14.

1. What are some ways people are able to work from home? _____

2. What are some ways people are able to engage in leisure-time activities at work? _____

3. What's the author's point of view in the article? _____

4. Do you agree with the author's point of view? Why or why not? _____

16 **WHAT ABOUT YOU?** Look at the list of technological tools below. First, circle the ones you have or use. Then indicate how difficult it would be for you to live without each.

How difficult would it be to live without _____?	not difficult at all	somewhat difficult	extremely difficult
a cell phone	○	○	○
a tablet	○	○	○
a laptop	○	○	○
e-mail	○	○	○
the Internet	○	○	○
texting	○	○	○
a smart watch	○	○	○

According to some estimates, 65 percent of employees go online at work for personal, not work-related purposes every day. Of employees between the ages of 18 and 33, the number goes up to 73 percent.

Of the technological tools listed, which would be the most difficult for you to live without? Why?

_____

_____

LESSON 4

17 Place each of the activities in one of the categories below.

bungee jumping	mountain biking	surfing
extreme skiing	rock climbing	waterfall jumping
hang gliding	skydiving	white water rafting

I've already done it.	I can't wait to try it.	It could be fun.	Not a chance!

W104   UNIT 10

18 Take the quiz to see if you have a risk-taking personality.

QUIZ Are you a risk taker or a risk avoider?
www.adventurequiz.com

1 Which type of movie would you rather watch?
a. scary
b. funny

2 Which would you rather do at an amusement park?
a. go on a roller coaster
b. see a show

3 Which sentence describes you better?
a. I love trying new things.
b. I prefer to stick close to home.

4 Which genre of music would you rather listen to?
a. urban dance
b. pop

5 What kind of clothes do you wear? Pick one adjective from each pair.
a. trendy   a. flashy   a. wild
b. classic   b. subdued   b. conservative

6 Which do you prefer? Pick one choice from each pair.
a. to stand out in a crowd   a. fast-paced city life
b. to conform   b. slower pace of the country or suburbs

7 What are your shopping habits?
a. impulse buying
b. comparison shopping

8 How do you spend your free time?
a. I find something exciting to do.
b. I catch up on work and chores.

9 Which would you rather take up?
a. karate
b. quilting

10 Pick the adjective or phrase that best describes you from each of the following pairs.
a. thrill-seeking   a. rebellious   a. aggressive   a. adventurous
b. conservative   b. obedient   b. cautious   b. prefer routine

a. a troublemaker   a. self-confident   a. energetic   a. outgoing
b. well-behaved   b. nervous   b. calm   b. shy

Count up your score.

How many a's did you check? _____

How many b's did you check? _____

0–5 a answers: You probably have a "small t" personality. You don't like thrills and prefer to avoid them. You're among the faint of heart. You prefer certainty and routine. But don't get too set in your ways. A little adventure from time to time would do you some good.

6–11 a answers: You fall somewhere in the middle of the risk-taking continuum. You're probably willing to take some risks from time to time, but maybe prefer to avoid risk in general. Sounds like you live a pretty balanced life.

12–20 a answers: You probably have a "big T" personality. You love thrills and can't get enough of them. You're happiest living on the edge. You like to take risks and do new things. Remember: risk-taking can be the key to success, but it can also get you into trouble. Make an effort to exercise some caution.

How do your quiz results compare with your answer to Exercise E on Student's Book page 119? If they differ, which do you think is more accurate? Explain.

_____

_____

19 Complete each sentence with an adverb of manner. Form adverbs from the adjectives in the box.

| beautiful | lucky | quiet | safe |
| confident | physical | sad | |

1. Loraine spoke _____ about her plans for the future.
2. She went skydiving yesterday and landed _____, I'm happy to say.
3. There were no survivors of the plane crash, _____.
4. I fell when I was rock climbing, but _____, I wasn't hurt.
5. Luke sang _____ last night.
6. Checking your devices before bed can affect you _____.
7. Lin walked as _____ as she could, so she wouldn't wake anyone.

> ". . . it is uninteresting to do easy things. We find out about ourselves
> only when we take risks, when we challenge and question."
> — Magdalena Abakanowicz, Polish artist, born 1930

GRAMMAR BOOSTER

A Rewrite each statement, using <u>be supposed to</u>.

1. Everyone says windsurfing is hard to learn. _____
2. My friends all think that movie is horrible. _____
3. Everyone says the new CEO is a tyrant. _____
4. They say that border collies are extremely intelligent dogs. _____
5. It's said that playing piano makes you better at math. _____
6. I've never been to Hawaii, but everyone says it's beautiful. _____
7. My friends all thought the book was better than the movie, but I thought the movie was better.
_____

B Decide how <u>would</u> is used in each sentence. Write the letter on the line.

a. to express past repeated or habitual actions
b. as the past form of the future with <u>will</u>
c. to express past intentions or plans that changed
d. for polite requests in the present or future
e. to express a present or future result of an unreal condition

_____ 1. We would just sit and talk for hours when we were younger.
_____ 2. Jan thought she would become a doctor, but she ended up being a teacher.
_____ 3. Lauren promised she would pick me up on time.
_____ 4. Ellie, would you please help me with my homework?
_____ 5. If Melissa didn't work so hard, she would have more time to relax.
_____ 6. I wouldn't go skydiving even if you paid me.
_____ 7. My dad would read stories to us every night.
_____ 8. Ron said he would read the book on vacation.
_____ 9. Tania said, "Would you please hurry up?"
_____ 10. I didn't think I would like that play, but I was wrong. It was great!
_____ 11. You wouldn't be scared of the water if you knew how to swim.
_____ 12. Our class would go on a trip together every year.

C Rewrite the sentences using the adverb of manner in parentheses.

1. Monet's paintings are beautiful. (incredibly) _____
2. Ella answered her phone. (angrily) _____
3. Our new employee always works. (hard) _____
4. Bill asked Ty not to smoke. (politely) _____
5. That new sports car is fast. (unbelievably) _____
6. She waved when she saw her friend. (happily) _____
7. She walked away. (slowly) _____
8. David remembered that he needed to call his sister. (suddenly) _____

D Write your own sentences, using the adverbs in parentheses.

1. (well) _____
2. (poorly) _____
3. (suddenly) _____
4. (sadly) _____
5. (slowly) _____

WRITING: Presenting and supporting opinions clearly

A **PREWRITING: T-CHART** Go back to the article "Work at Home, Play at Work" on page 103. Reread the article and underline sentences that you agree or disagree with. Then write notes on the T-chart. You can quote the author or paraphrase. See the model on the right.

agree	disagree
I agree that technology has allowed people to engage in leisure time activities at work. Many people use the Internet at work for personal reasons.	I don't think working from home is a bad thing. It is good for employees to have a little flexibility.
The writer mentions "a definite separation of work and home life." I agree that this is missing in today's world.	

agree	disagree

B **WRITING** Write a critique of the article. State your own opinion at the beginning. Then use the notes from your T-chart to support your point of view.

_____
_____
_____
_____
_____
_____
_____
_____
_____
_____
_____
_____
_____
_____

C **SELF-CHECK**

☐ Did I use connecting words and phrases to present and support my opinions?
☐ Did I use quotation marks when citing the writer's own words?
☐ Did I paraphrase the writer's words when I didn't use direct speech?